Teaching Notes on Piano Examination Pieces 1999–2000

CU00482256

Grades 1–7

CLARA TAYLOR
LRAM, ARAM, FRSA

Chief Examiner of
The Associated Board of the Royal Schools of Music

ANTHONY WILLIAMS
M.Mus, Dip.RAM, GRSM, LRAM

Head of Keyboard and Assistant Director of Music at Radley College

Teaching Notes on Piano Examination Pieces 1999–2000

Grades 1–7

The Associated Board of the Royal Schools of Music

First published in 1998 by
The Associated Board of the Royal Schools of Music (Publishing) Ltd
14 Bedford Square, London WC1B 3JG

© 1998 by The Associated Board of the Royal Schools of Music

ISBN 1 86096 058 8

AB 2687

All rights reserved. No part of this publication may be reproduced,
stored in a retrieval system, or transmitted in any form or by any
means, electronic, mechanical, photocopying, recording, or otherwise,
without the prior permission of the copyright owner.

Printed in Great Britain by Caligraving Limited, Thetford, Norfolk

CONTENTS

INTRODUCTION

Teachers reading the commentaries and general hints in this booklet will realize that they were written with personal understanding of the many challenges that teachers face. Having taught at all levels, from beginners to diploma standard, Anthony Williams and I are very much aware of the skill, patience and insight needed to help average pupils along the way. Musically talented, motivated children are a joy and present fewer difficulties to their fortunate teachers but these pupils are in a minority. The Associated Board's system of grades is for the benefit of all levels of ability and was originally intended for those who form the vast majority of candidates heard in exams throughout the world.

The exciting increase in the number of pieces for each grade not only enlivens the teacher's work but also makes it possible to find a programme that really suits each individual candidate. Do explore the pieces that are not printed in the graded albums; these are easily obtainable and there are some wonderful choices in these lists that might otherwise be missed. In the commentaries we hope to have given sufficient guidance to enable you to suit the pieces to your own students with even more awareness and confidence than before. The first essential in starting a new piece is the desire to learn it. Once a pupil's interest is caught, the business of managing the musical and technical essentials becomes purposeful and more easily sustained. We have tried to suggest angles of approach, especially in repertoire that does not have an imaginative title. So often it is the way in which the music is introduced to the pupil that influences the effort that follows and we have often given priority to these considerations.

In giving information about phrasing, dynamics and fingering, we stress that these are suggestions based on experience. Teachers will all have their own ideas and we have tried to avoid being fussily prescriptive. In the choice of fingering in particular, so much depends on each individual pupil and the final question to ask will always be: 'Does it work easily and create the right musical effect?'

Perhaps it should be emphasized that in pointing out what examiners will be listening for we are only suggesting ways of benefiting the music. Anything that improves the performance is bound to be welcomed in the exam and it is, after all, the standard of playing and love of music that count in the long run.

It may be useful to consider the following areas in more detail.

TEMPO

Slow practice is often essential but it pays to keep the final performing tempo of the piece in mind. Sometimes pupils get stuck at a slow pace, use too heavy a touch and find it difficult to achieve the fluency and vitality of faster repertoire. Cautious players need particular encouragement and plenty of demonstration to give a clear sound picture of the intended speed. The same applies to scales and arpeggios, where an even tone and a good flowing tempo are both important.

RUBATO

This is an unmistakable element in musical phrasing but can also be encouraged by explanation to less-naturally-aware pupils. In Classical or earlier styles, the small fluctuations are within the bar and need to be very subtle indeed to avoid upsetting the basic pulse. Phrasing in these styles is shown more effectively by the use of tone, gently emphasizing the main points and being aware of the rise and fall of the pitch. *Rubato* in Romantic styles shapes the phrases by moving towards the main peak, then relaxing afterwards. Pupils are often better at making a *ritardando* than at getting faster but both forms of movement are needed to create balanced phrasing. Picking up the tempo after a *ritardando* is also a skill that needs awareness. Pencilling in arrows pointing forwards and backwards in the music is often a helpful way of giving visual clues and encouraging the pupil to look ahead. Even experienced pianists sometimes do this and youngsters who are struggling with the notes certainly need extra guidance to keep the whole phrase structure in mind.

PEDALLING

Teachers will find some pedalling marked in early grade pieces but *legato* pedalling is not really required until around Grades 4 or 5. Pupils are often fascinated with the effect of using the sustaining pedal and finding the right places in early grades to begin to use this skill is an opportunity not to be missed. The co-ordination of foot and hands in *legato* pedalling usually takes longer to acquire but is necessary for much of the piano repertoire beyond Grade 4. It is important to keep the heel on the floor when pedalling, using only the toes and front sole of the foot, rather than the whole leg, which causes tension in the muscles. When pedalling becomes natural, it can be safely put on 'auto pilot', providing the pupil is always listening carefully to avoid over-generous pedalling with a blurred result.

EDITIONS

There is often concern about editorial suggestions in early music and the realization of ornaments. In the early grades the editor has followed markings given by the composer and sometimes added further articulation marks or dynamics, in keeping with the style and period. The footnotes give details of which marks are the composer's and which are editorial. At the higher grades there are fewer marks on the music itself but the footnotes give suggestions for phrasing and articulation. When the dynamics are only editorial suggestions, they do not have to be slavishly followed. All music needs dynamic colour and the use of this is purely subjective. Phrasing will inevitably cause dynamic fluctuations, apart from the higher or lower levels of sound that may be chosen for a longer section. In the more contemporary pieces, the musical markings are usually the composer's and should be incorporated into the performance for an authentic account.

ORNAMENTS

The Associated Board prints the following advice to teachers:

> Where appropriate, pieces have been checked with original source material and edited as necessary for instructional purposes. Fingering, phrasing, bowing, metronome marks and the editorial realization of ornaments (where given) are for guidance but are not comprehensive or obligatory.

Ornaments are just another aspect of the performance. If it is possible for them to be incorporated comfortably into the rhythm of the piece, they are always welcome as an additional aspect of the style. If playing the suggested ornament is going to upset the pulse, then it is much better to shorten the ornament into a turn or mordent, or to leave it out entirely to keep the structure of the piece intact. It is at Grade 6 that pieces really requiring ornamentation should only be chosen when the ornaments can be incorporated, even if in modified form. In the lower grades examiners are happy to accept performances without ornaments, providing that other musical aspects, such as phrasing and dynamics, have been given consideration.

THE SUPPORTING TESTS

Scales – Key sense and agility are both developed gradually with the requirements throughout the grades. An even, rhythmic finger touch with

3

smoothly incorporated thumb turns is a vital technical basis. Arpeggios help pupils to become much more familiar with the extent of the keyboard and also develop chord awareness. Keeping elbows a little away from the sides avoids the bumps and sudden lurches that sometimes get in the way of a fluent progression through the octaves. Co-ordination is essential and, as in everything else, an inner rhythm needs to underpin these technical requirements. Contrary scales also help independence of hands. Different rhythmic patterns, dynamics and forms of articulation all add to the pianist's control of tone, which is the musical equivalent of an artist's palette of colours.

Sight-reading – The examiner will give the candidate 30 seconds to try out and look carefully through the sight-reading test. Many candidates are too shy to actually play parts of the test but this is strongly to be encouraged, to give confidence to the attempt. The first essential is to set up a basic rhythm and to count out the structure of the first bar or so in order to give the time-values real meaning. The time-honoured words 'Keep going' still apply and pupils should learn to ignore notation mistakes and press on in their chosen tempo, regardless of accidents along the way. Examiners consider key sense and rhythm equally and appreciate courageous attempts to keep the piece in shape. So often candidates will falter or stop when a mistake occurs which could easily be overcome with a different approach. The eventual value of adequate sight-reading far outweighs the difficulties of acquiring it in the early stages.

Aural tests – These days teachers are frequently including aural tests during the course of a lesson, using phrases to be sung or clapped that are met in the pieces. The various skills that are developed by these tests help an all-round awareness of music, and the D test, recognizing various aspects of a short piece played by the examiner, is particularly valuable for mature listening and appreciation. Many candidates and teachers worry about the singing tests but it is recognition of pitch and intervals that is being assessed, not vocal quality. Humming, singing an octave lower or whistling are perfectly acceptable ways of responding. The C test in lower grades can be answered by clapping or singing the change, putting up a hand when the difference happens or explaining it in simple terms. It is not necessary to give exact rhythm or pitch changes; the usual answers are in this style, 'It went faster after the first note' or 'The last-but-one note was lower'.

Teachers with limited piano skills often use recordings to help with the last test; sometimes the examples can be put on tape by a helpful colleague. The current aural tests are producing higher marks than the previous set and most pupils can manage at least some parts. Examiners assess the response as a whole, so if one test is a regular problem, it is only a small part of this section and should not be allowed to become out of proportion in the pupil's mind.

Finally, here are a few general observations which have proved their worth over the years:

- In order to have a clear idea of what examiners are looking for, refer to the Board's Basis of Assessment, which is printed in *These Music Exams*. This gives a guide as to how examiners award marks for the pieces and which elements in the playing contribute to the different categories: Pass, Merit and Distinction.
- All the sections of the exam are individually assessed positively or negatively from the Pass mark. Marks are not added from zero or deducted from the total.
- Careful selection of the pieces makes all the difference to the preparation period. This is now much easier with the increased choice in the new lists.
- Aim to be ready for the exam a few weeks before the expected date. Gradual preparation is essential for reliability on the Big Day.
- Incorporate scales, sight-reading and aural in small doses in most lessons, extracting suitable material from current pieces as well as using the specimen tests.
- A positive attitude to nerves and realistic hopes will create a more helpful climate than over-optimistic expectations. All candidates feel a degree of nervousness and examiners understand this natural response. They will assess the playing on the day with accuracy, giving detailed comments on what occurs, but will also be alert to signs of musicality and achievement which still show despite anxious slips or hesitations.
- Playing to friends and parents builds confidence and this performance practice helps to make the point that musicians, even professionals, rarely live up to their own expectations. It is the effort that goes into the attempt which counts at all levels and foothills are essential on the way to greater heights.

GRADE 1

The first exam is potentially an exciting event and the choice of pieces is crucial, as pupils will probably be living with the programme for longer than any previous repertoire. In the early grades, basic accuracy of notes and time at a suitable tempo will achieve a Pass. More musical interest and character in the piece will attract Merit marks but really polished playing will be needed for a Distinction. Serious errors will, of course, lower the category of the marks but examiners are well aware of the human element and balance the positive and negative qualities of the whole performance, rather than focusing on any isolated aspect. You will find further information in the Basis of Assessment printed in the new edition of *These Music Exams*.

The wider choice gives a much better chance to match the pieces to the player and the following overview should help to simplify the initial exploration of the lists.

LIST A

All the pieces are very approachable in terms of notes and time. The Bach 'Aria in F' is a little more technically awkward than it looks and the Neefe 'Allegretto in C' has one challenge in the second line but these are well within the level of the grade. Lifting the performance in this list will require some control and awareness of articulation, phrasing and dynamics, as well as an underlying buoyancy in the rhythm.

LIST B

A *legato* touch and sense of shape are often important in these expressive pieces. Those with the easiest notes often need even more sense of shape and mood – 'The Pear Tree is Laden with Fruit' by Alwyn and the 'Arioso in F' by Türk are particular examples. The piece by Henkel is at the harder end of the level of difficulty but musically so worthwhile and 'Cuckoo' needs careful rhythm but otherwise there are no hidden hazards.

LIST C

Several of the more outgoing pieces need a good rhythmic sense. 'Calypso Joe', 'The Swinging Sioux' and 'Jamaican Rumba' all need a sense of fun but contain some musical medicine in the time values. 'Calypso Joe' is probably the easiest of this set. The 'Bagatelle No. 4' and 'Friday' will suit pupils who are more at home with thoughtful introspective moods.

A:1 J. C. Bach *Aria in F*

This is a lyrical, tuneful aria and one of the lesser-known pieces from the *Anna Magdalena Bach Book*. It was written by one of her sons for his brothers and sisters to play or sing.

It needs a *cantabile* right hand, as the title suggests, but think of it also as a slow dance in two-in-a-bar, keeping the crotchet upbeats lightly detached and encouraging an effective *decrescendo* at the ends of phrases.

Consider the fingering carefully as it is technically a little more awkward than it looks. Anticipate a few uneasy jumps from small hands, which could result in an accent in the right hand on the second beat of bar 2 and in extra time being taken at the double bar and the change of hand position in bar 11. A detached crotchet in the left hand (bars 8 and 9) will also help avoid an off-beat accent, easing the jump.

Detaching the first two crotchets in bars 7, 11 etc will give the piece more buoyancy and the editorial dynamics will give excellent scope for musical interest. Be aware that Bach's *staccato* wedges in bars 12 and 14 merely indicate that the minims should be important (perhaps pompous) and separated, not accented. A little *ritardando* through the final three crotchets will help finish the Aria with charm.

A:2 Clementi *Arietta in C*

This is a cheerful song with a rather cheeky end to the fourth line. There is plenty of scope for improvising some suitable words to the melody, helping the pupil to shape the line naturally and to think through the phrases. The piece should cause few problems technically; it falls easily under small hands and there are no awkward jumps. There are, however, just one or two moments from bar 13 onwards where attention to the fingering will be needed to ease the way.

Sensitive shaping will be the essence of an effective and musical performance. Think, perhaps, of two separate phrases in the first line, one long phrase through the second line and then a *crescendo* through to bar 11, thereafter following Clementi's own markings. The left hand can help here, particularly in bars 6 to 12, where it can help keep musical direction through the right-hand rests (bars 8–10), though do keep the repeated G light, leading with the upper note. In bar 6 the repeated notes in the right hand will need to be phrased carefully, lightening the final two. Listen out for any unwanted accent on the second beat of bars 2 and 4.

Finally, enjoy the wonderful dissonance of the D♯ in bar 17 and keep the final semiquavers even and controlled, though a nicely judged *ritardando* would give an effective end to the performance.

A:3 Anon. *Menuet in F*

This charming menuet is from a musical notebook put together by Leopold Mozart for his eight-year-old daughter Nannerl and subsequently played by Wolfgang at the age of four! The first bars are deceptively easy; the last few bars of each line, however, will require a little more attention. Choose the tempo carefully; the elegance could be easily lost if it is too slow and effective shaping of the repeated notes made quite hard.

As the piece divides, perhaps too easily, into two-bar phrases it may help the musical interest to think of the final four bars of each line as one phrase. Keep the upbeats light and crotchets generally detached, though you may wish to phrase the left hand with the right hand in bars 1, 3, 5, 7 etc, if the *staccato/legato* contrast proves awkward. Detaching the final left-hand crochet in bar 15 from the first in bar 16 will allow the left-hand 5th finger to jump to the F should you wish but, in general, give the written fingering a try as it presents a good solution to a few awkward shifts.

An effective performance will include some convincing dynamic contrast, a sensitive balance between the hands and some well-shaped phrasing, with a lightening of the touch through the repeated notes. Be aware of the jump between the two sections – little hands will have to move quickly to avoid extra beats.

The final triplet needs to flow naturally. Don't labour the tempo here but do relax it through the final crotchets to bring the dance gracefully to a close.

A:4 Graupner *Bourrée in D minor*

The description, 'A French dance of the 17th century', may not fill your pupils with an immediate desire to learn this bourrée but a picture of a beautiful ballroom and the clothes of the period may well set light to the imagination.

The tempo of this piece should be two stately steps to a bar, at around minim = 72. Four-bar phrases that lean on 'feminine' endings, in which the final beat of the phrase is lifted gently, contrast with the straightforward endings of the second and fourth phrases. As in all dances, the rhythm is all-important and the pulse should be strongly held across all bar lines right to the end of the final phrase.

The only obvious tonal contrast is in the second phrase. It would be a pity to miss this chance of variety and to play the entire piece at the same dynamic level. The slurs help to give an elegant style and, as well as those marked, try adding them at bars 9, 10, 11, 12, where the implication is similar. This may sound like a fussy detail but it is only a matter of leaning slightly on the first of the paired notes and lifting the second – quite easy physically but valuable in adding that certain something to the phrasing. The left hand need not be left out, for at bars 4, 8 and 16 the last two crotchets could be detached if you like the effect. If this proves too complicated, *legato* crotchets will also work well if phrased off from the first beat in the bar. You could perhaps describe these details of phrasing to your pupils as the musical equivalent of a lace frill around the cuff of a 17th-century shirt. The minor key should not cause a sad impression; after all, this is a courtly dance.

A:5 Neefe *Allegretto in C*

The straightforward appearance of the opening four bars will encourage many teachers to look hopefully ahead only to see hazards in bars 6 and 7. Do the ornaments have to be played? Will my pupils be penalized for leaving them out? This is only Grade 1! These heartfelt cries are heard at most teachers' seminars and need to be answered clearly and reassuringly.

These tiny mordents add attractive decoration but are only that – just frills. If your pupil can manage them deftly, starting on the beat for full stylish effect, the phrase will have extra interest but there are other ways of catching the style. Try playing just the second mordent each time (bars 7 and 23) or leave the ornaments out if they cause hesitations or stumbles. Showing the phrase points by leaning on the first beats and lifting the second in bars 8, 16 and 24 will give the right graceful effect and is fundamentally more important to the shape of the phrases than the ornaments.

The smaller phrasing details – the detached first quavers, followed by three slurred ones – may be too much for some pupils to manage but the dynamics, especially when shown in each hand, give plenty of colour and a conversational feel, as if two people were chatting pleasantly together, exchanging ideas. The only other technical concern is in the second line. This is best practised in two-bar sections, with a quick glance at the keys for changes of position.

There is a welcome bonus to pupils learning this piece, as they will notice when they have learnt the notes of the second line that the third line is the same as the first. Examiners will be especially interested to hear performances where this third line is played with a different feel from that of the opening and where the last two bars are thoughtfully shaped.

A:6 Telemann *Gavotte in C*

Girls often respond more naturally to a *grazioso* indication than boys but there are ways to help a performance that may sound rather stolid for this early dance. It all lies in the handling of the opening four crotchets and the same pattern when it reappears. If the first two crotchets are lightly detached and lead to an accented first beat of the next bar, the main rhythmic characteristic will be in place and the essential vitality will be much easier to carry through the rest of the dance.

Marking up the four-bar phrases in practice sections makes the piece immediately approachable and there is plenty of repetition in the writing, which is always encouraging to beginners learning a new piece. As it should not take too long to make friends with the notes, the dynamics can be included at an early stage. The middle section from bars 8–12 starts with a stronger colour and then there is a sudden drop to *piano* for the brief moment in A minor.

It is always good to hear young players who have the control to play *legato* in one hand and *staccato* in the other and there are several chances to show off this skill.

The phrasing structure helps players to think across the bar lines and set up a regular basic beat, which is probably the most important form of musical awareness that can be encouraged at this early stage.

B:1 Alwyn *The Pear Tree is Laden with Fruit*

The imaginative title conjures up images of a warm, autumnal afternoon and heavy, gently swaying branches, suggesting an unhurried tempo.

The piece shouldn't present too many technical challenges and indeed the first two bars of the piece fall easily under five fingers and are repeated three times. The fingering will play a vital part in bar 12, persuading the hand to go to the different phrase ending, and the pause gives time to move the hands to the new position in bar 13.

The main challenges, however, are in creating an effective mood and eloquently shaping the phrases as marked. A rich (juicy) tone in bars 8 and 13 and an elegantly-shaped right-hand melody will enhance the performance, keeping the left hand unobtrusive and calm. As always, explore the dynamic contrast. The crotchet rest in bar 8 will give time to prepare a sensitive *pianissimo* – and why not allow more confident pupils to try some *una corda* in bar 9?

A larger pupil might consider using some pedal to warm up the final two bars and a well-judged *ritardando* at the end will confirm an effective performance.

B:2 Le Couppey *Melody in C*

The opening to this piece is full of smiles and playground games, with a wonderful, contrasting and slightly moodier middle section. Younger pupils might like to make up a suitable story to help encourage even more musical interest.

The murmuring left-hand quavers will need to be well controlled and rhythmically even to avoid the accompaniment becoming too strident. Keep the quavers lighter as the arpeggios ascend, the arm relaxed and fingers close to the keys. More confident pianists might also consider a less articulated sound, releasing the bottom note a little later to enhance the harmonies. The left hand needs to know instinctively where to move, so some practice playing it as chords will help, particularly in bars 4–5.

Project the attractive right-hand melody and give it plenty of musical shape. To avoid unwanted accents you will need to judge carefully the approach to the first note of each right-hand phrase, especially where it is preceded by a jump or change of finger (bars 5 and 13). There is plenty of dynamic variety marked: aim for a whispering *pianissimo* and a good, contrasting *mezzoforte* in the middle section.

Finally, remember the *da capo* and allow a small *ritardando* in the final bar to bring the melody to a gentle conclusion.

B:3 Türk *Arioso in F*

Playing the notes of this beautiful arioso will present few problems but an effective performance will need sensitive shaping of the right-hand melody and a good *cantabile* tone. Think of each phrased couplet as a written-out appoggiatura, relaxing into the first note and lifting gently on the second, and avoid accenting the third beat of bars 6 and 14, following the jump. The suggested, unhurried tempo will help the tonal control and a good range of dynamic will enhance the musical interest but be careful not to force the *forte* tone in such a thin texture.

Use the left-hand rests to get the hand ready (bars 5–6 and 13–14). Avoid labouring the tempo at the suggested ornament (bar 15); try keeping the hand light and arm relaxed to free the fingers but if it continues to distort the line it is probably better left out.

Finally, notice the editorial ⌒ at the end: it enhances the final bar but, more practically, may stop a nervous, panicked rush into the next piece.

B:4 Breslaur *Cuckoo*

It is unusual to hear a cuckoo answered by a perfect fifth! You would normally expect the left hand to mimic the right hand but here the bird seems to be only in the treble clef.

It is important to play all the *staccato* notes with the same crispness in each hand. After some weeks of playing this piece, pupils may not realize that familiarity has tended to make the second crotchets become longer and this would lose much of the contrast between the *staccato* and *legato*. The dynamics suggest a loud cuckoo in the right hand, followed by a quieter echo also in the right hand, when the same notes are repeated. On a strange piano this might not always come off as planned, so it would be a good idea to play another piece before this one in the actual exam.

The *allegretto* crotchet = 132 works well and at this speed it is still possible to slip in the triplet neatly, which is the only potential stumbling block in the piece. Examiners will be pleased by exact time values here as the triplets could easily be too slow or played as two semiquavers and a quaver instead of three even notes within the one crotchet beat left in the bar. Once this is mastered, the piece trips along with few hazards and plenty of outdoor charm.

B:5 H. Henkel *Piano Piece for the Young*

Pupils who respond to a lovely melody will be attracted by this wistful, elegant piece. It is at the harder end of the level of difficulty for the grade but so easy on the ear, if not the fingers, that the effort to master it will be well worthwhile.

Separate-hand practice will be necessary, so to offset any potential boredom, why not offer to play the missing part during lessons? This would remind the pupil of the final musical effect while still enabling them to think of one hand at a time.

Once the notes are fairly reliable, a slightly more flowing tempo than the suggested crotchet = 58 might help the graceful phrasing and will also encourage a lilting two-in-a-bar. Both hands are *legato* but the left hand should accompany the melody, keeping just a little below the dynamic level of the right hand. Pupils with a good physical memory will find that this piece is extremely rewarding and quite reliable under exam conditions, despite the early struggle to get the notes 'into the fingers'.

All dynamics and phrasing suggested by the editor are very helpful in giving shape and character to this slightly sad piece, which could sound simply a pretty tune. The ornaments could be left out if they cause any un-evenness in the melody. There are plenty of challenges to be mastered of long-term musical worth, which matter at this stage rather more than the grace notes, although they do give that extra polish when managed fluently.

B:6 Sartorio *Who is there?*

A quiet word of warning before pupils start to learn this piece will prevent them beginning the left hand in the bass clef and spending a week creating the wrong habits and some puzzling sounds. A brisk, cheerful tempo is suggested but the semiquavers need to be evenly controlled, so a faster speed than crotchet = 116 may be unwise.

Once the notes are known, it would be fun, and a good aural test, to play the opening call and ask your pupil to sing the answering phrase, then to reverse the pattern. The notes are not difficult to learn or play but the detail, such as *staccato* in one hand and *legato* in the other, can be a challenge to those who do not yet have a sense of how each hand is playing as well as which notes are being struck.

The *ritardando* followed by *a tempo* at bars 17–18 will tell the examiner quite a lot about the pupil, as shaping this moment takes either very careful preparation, or a natural musical ability to allow a tempo to slacken then resume the earlier speed. The ending suggests that the caller eventually finds his friend and all is well.

It would be worth checking that your pupil can find the right octave even on a strange piano for the start of this piece, as it would be all too easy to begin an octave too low with very different musical effects!

C:1 Richard Rodney Bennett *Friday*

This piece sums up well what many of us may feel about Fridays. The wonderful cello-like tune in the opening suggests the end of a rather tiring week but the brighter middle section anticipates the weekend to come.

The opening needs a rich, *cantabile* tone and all the phrases benefit from plenty of dynamic shape and a real *legato*. Don't start too softly as there is a *pianissimo* to come at the end and grade the *crescendo* carefully so the tone doesn't become too bright from bar 13 onwards. A relaxed right-hand wrist will help the sound here.

Most of the piece falls kindly under the fingers, although try a left-hand 2nd finger instead of a 4th in bar 8 to avoid an awkward stretch. Control of the thirds (bars 13–16 etc) and projection of the left-hand melody (bars 9–12) may need a little work but the written fingering will guide the hand through the less comfortable stretches or changes of position. Try 4 and 2 instead of 2 and 1 in bar 24, separating slightly before the final phrase.

Make a little *rallentando* at the end and a good long pause, as though relaxing into an arm-chair for a well-earned rest.

C:2 Stephen Duro *Calypso Joe*

If your pupil has never been to the Caribbean, suggest to the parents that they take you both to Jamaica to absorb the atmosphere: sun, coconuts and exotic cocktails will all be part of essential exam preparation!

The effectiveness of this jaunty calypso will rely on a secure, steady rhythm, good attention to phrasing and a sense of fun. The notes aren't difficult and the repeated-note fingering will help guarantee reliable, clean articulation, although it may feel a little unnatural at first. Encourage an effective syncopation throughout; this will be enhanced by shortening the first-beat crotchet (bars 1, 3 etc), the B♭ (bars 2, 6 etc) and observing the rests. There is a danger of the left hand becoming too heavy; keep it buoyant and light and try an even broader range of dynamics than those marked.

The piece can work at a fairly moderate tempo but try the lively tempo marking; it will bring the piece to life and have the examiner up and swinging his or her hips.

C:3 William Gillock *The Swinging Sioux*

The Sioux are a Native American people who were buffalo hunters living in the heartland of the northern Great Plains before the arrival of white settlers. I suspect there weren't too many boogying to the sound of this tune but the comic image will prove popular with the young.

The piece uses the piano imaginatively, presents few challenges of balance and may be a very good choice for a more nervous pupil, who should be able to relax and enjoy the fun.

The performance needs to be absolutely rhythmical, with all the rests observed. Well-executed *staccato* left-hand chords will add to the rhythmic energy. Use a broad range of dynamics and shorten the final note of the phrase in bar 3 etc to highlight the accented As. Pupils will enjoy holding the pedal throughout bars 13–14 for the 'smoke signal', though they will need to prepare their hands in plenty of time to ensure the pulse doesn't slow here. Similarly, practise getting the right hand ready during the rest in bar 23 and both hands ready for the leap just before the final bar to avoid any hesitation.

Finally, aim for 'heap big dynamic contrast', particularly the surprise *fortissimo* at the end after the *diminuendo*, which should aim to surprise an unsuspecting buffalo or listener.

C:4 Hans-Günther Allers *Bagatelle No.4*

A title chosen by your pupil or yourself will help to give this piece the expressiveness it needs. This is an ideal chance to encourage pupils to listen to their own playing, especially to the tone colour, and to begin to be aware of joining and grading the sounds into smooth phrases. It will delight the examiner to hear the notes immediately after the right-hand ties evenly graded, rather than bumped into life. The directions 'slowly and expressively' help to suggest a quiet, walking tempo, which should be kept steady, particularly at bars 1, 8, 9 and 10, where pupils in a hurry will probably cut short the crotchet beats. Vertical lines are an effective visual reminder to count, or better still, to feel the beats.

As the left-hand chords need to last long enough to support the melody, the tone could be a little warmer than the *pianissimo* suggests. This will also avoid those disconcerting 'misfires' in an exam, when the notes fail to speak.

The range of dynamics is quite restrained and the phrasing of the melody ideally needs an imaginative freedom within the triplet patterns. Singing the melody while playing will help to catch the style.

The musical markings, such as the long tied As, the *crescendo* and *diminuendo*, the quiet dynamic range and the final, thoughtful pause, all need a player who will take trouble over these details and who will enjoy the subtle sounds that can be created with gentle care.

C:5 arr. Pauline Hall *Jamaican Rumba*

Some teachers will have played the original solo or two-piano version of this well-known piece and either a demonstration or a recording will be helpful in creating the enthusiasm to master the left-hand rhythm against the *legato* right-hand melody. Pupils could find this awkward, unless they have a 'sound picture' and a feel for the rhythm. It you can dance a rumba with your pupil it would certainly make the lesson memorable but the essential beat could also be found by using some suitable, fun words, such as 'fried bananas'. Separate practice, followed by the pupil managing one hand while you play the other, will probably be a necessary step to securing the co-ordination.

The right-hand melody is *legato* throughout and needs a lean on the main points of phrases, which are surprisingly classical in length and shape, peaking on the first beats of bars 8, 11, 15 and 19. The left hand could be all *legato*, or the third and fourth beats in each bar could be detached if the pupil has a good sense of rhythmic bite.

The *piano* phrase in bars 13–16 is a good chance for contrast, as the rest is all quite positive. Examiners will also appreciate a less obtrusive bass line, which allows the strong melody to come across with clarity and spirit, without causing the tone to become hard. The final chord is best held only for its exact length, rather like a final gesture in the dance or 'olé'.

C:6 Feliks Rybicki *Cat and Mouse*

The two characters spring off the page here and it is easy to imagine the timid mouse with its light *staccato* chords and the threatening cat with its A minor 'five finger exercise' quavers – a wonderful way of making dynamics and articulation come to life.

Take care that the right sharps are played. At a quick glance the D♯ could be mis-read in the left-hand chords and some pupils will tend to cut short the rests or extend them while searching for the next position. The rhythm is a vital part of this piece and the rests provide a useful moment to leap across the keyboard at fast changes of position such as at bars 8–9. It will be essential to look at the keys if these leaps are to have secure and rhythmic landings.

The feel of two-in-a-bar will work at quite widely differing tempi but 'allegretto' suggests a minim of around 72, which helps the stealthy-footstep effect. The *accelerando* and pause create a wonderful picture of a chase, then a moment's suspense before the cat makes its final dramatic pounce.

GRADE 2

For those who have previously taken Grade 1, this experience of an exam will add insight to the selection of the pieces for the next grade. Teachers will remember which items were a particular success and will be able to select something similar for the next attempt. There is a great variety of choice within these lists and it would be good experience for your pupil to have three pieces in very different styles and moods to explore a wide span of expression.

LIST A

It's always encouraging to see great composers in the lists for early grades and here we have Purcell, Haydn and Beethoven, with their obvious advantages of content. The Beethoven sonatina movement is the most demanding in terms of musical maturity and the Daquin is a little easier (but not for 'key huggers'). The Haydn scherzo movement is for those with neat fingerwork and the Purcell Hornpipe is ideal for rhythm-conscious pupils with a flair for detail.

LIST B

There are several melodic gems here. The Gurlitt 'Serenade in B flat' and Somervell 'Plaintive Waltz' have obvious appeal and the Reinecke 'Prelude' gives the chance for left-hand expressiveness. Breslaur's 'A Romp' is likely to be reasonably trouble free and the Kirchner 'Poco Vivace in C' is also great fun but rather more demanding, with its quick jumps.

LIST C

Several strongly atmospheric pieces feature in this list, each with a clear mood and style. The gentler choices would be the Bartók 'Romanian Christmas Carol' or the Kabalevsky, both imaginative and potentially poetic. Extroverts will go for 'Beanery Boogie' or 'Cakes and Ale', and 'Little Mouse' is not as tricky as it looks.

A:1 Hässler *Ecossaise in G*

Finding the first note will be the first challenge. This looks a long way up from the last familiar F on the stave and examiners will probably hear a few performances that begin in the wrong octave! An ecossaise is a form of dance but this piece looks rather like tripping down stairs and this might be an enjoyable way to think of the lightness needed for the detached notes in the opening phrase. The *forte* is probably better thought of as bright or crisp playing, as it would be all too easy to make a thunderous descent.

Fortunately the *staccato* notes happen at the same time in each hand, which makes the co-ordination easier, but the left hand will need to be watched for any signs of forgotten rests. The *legato* thirds at bars 9 and 11 will need some separate practice and, although the printed fingering works well, if pupils prefer to use 3/1 then 2/1 in the chords of bar 10, there is no longer a belief that putting your thumb on a black key is a sin. Unconventional fingering is sometimes necessary to achieve a desired musical effect. The semiquaver scale passages lie comfortably under the hand, so control should not be a problem here. The dynamic range is all quite positive, so it will make a welcome change to hear the start of the second section played at a noticeably quieter level than the beginning and end.

Repeats are not needed in exams. It is better to give a spirited performance at a lively pace once through, than risk repeating the sections with possibly less success.

A:2 Haydn *Scherzo*

Different patterns often result in different tempi and there is plenty of potential for a seasick basic beat in this otherwise happy piece.

Slowing down for the difficult bits is understandable but the rhythm *must* tick away evenly and broken chords and scales prove their worth yet again, as their well-known shapes are met in pieces such as this one. The main danger points are the opening F major bar and its reappearances and, even more so, the middle section, starting at bar 9, where cautious left-hand semiquavers could easily slow up the speed.

Pupils with good finger facility will enjoy showing off their technique and perhaps also begin to appreciate the pleasure of playing accurate, even notes at a brisk speed. The suggested tempo is fine for the playful title and the semiquavers will ripple along but a slightly faster speed will also be possible for the very competent and the brave.

This is not a piece to choose for those who struggle for agility, or who stick determinedly to a slow tempo out of anxiety. The semiquaver runs need even clarity and are best accompanied by lightly detached left-hand chords. A relaxed left-hand wrist will help the semiquavers at bar 9 to provide an even background to the quieter middle section, which is a real chance for effective contrast.

The classical four-bar phrasing needs emphasis at the main points and examiners will notice with pleasure if the left hand is also responding to dynamics and phrasing.

A:3 Purcell *Hornpipe in B flat*

One small boy recently thought a hornpipe was a kind of wind instrument. Modern children are usually unfamiliar with the sailors' crossed arms and almost Russian foot movements but the point to get across is that this is a dance and should be fun. The key signature and those dreaded ornaments will put off some pupils but there are plenty of advantages to consider when making this choice.

The melody is written by one of England's greatest composers and, even with the simple two-line texture, the quality of the melody is obvious. Helpful footnotes reassure us that Henry Purcell himself would probably have liked us to detach the quavers and also the left-hand crotchets, so no careful *legato* fingering is needed.

The ornaments give extra point to the peaks of phrases but this could also be done by leaning on these notes and lightening the following ones, if playing the full ornaments is beyond reach at this stage.

Examiners would always prefer to hear an easier version of the written-out trill, a mordent for instance, than a well-meaning but laboured attempt to play the full decoration, which upsets the rhythm.

Repeats are not required. It is a short piece and pupils will probably find it fun to try to keep the sailors dancing at exactly the same speed during the half a minute or so it takes to perform it.

A:4 attrib. Beethoven *Romanze*

Lyrical and cheerful music, this romanze should bring a smile to the face and be played with cheeky innocence. It is one of the longer pieces for the grade but is a very attractive choice and will richly reward the effort.

A natural flow and easy, lilting accompaniment is needed. Small hands may find the left-hand control less easy but keep the chords light and gently hold the bass notes to enhance the harmonies as Beethoven suggests.

Plenty of dynamic shaping to the melody will immediately capture the listener's (and examiner's) attention; the more musical and instinctive student may quite naturally linger a little at the top of the phrases and this will add to the charm. Make a feature of the chords and *crescendo* in bars 16–19 without forcing the tone and give the quavers an easy flexibility to introduce the return of the main tune in bars 20–21.

The repeated notes in the right hand are a potential hazard as they may become too strident: a light *staccato* and gentle *crescendo* through will help. The grace notes will also need to be kept light (with not too much arm weight) and the left-hand rests, without which the texture could become rather thick, must be observed.

Enjoy the slightly questioning beginning to the coda, where we briefly sense E minor, then finish with a joyful final few bars.

A:5 Daquin *Suite de la Réjouissance*

Those jazz-minded amongst your pupils will recognize a walking-bass pattern here and, once this left hand has been mastered, they too can join in the hunters' celebrations as there is little else of any major technical concern.

There are a few awkward corners where attention to the fingering will ease the way, especially bars 5 and 13 where, if the hands are big enough, it might help to put the 2nd finger on the right-hand B and thumb on the following C to set up the next phrase.

Practise the left-hand *legato* to help the fingers learn where they are going, though playing it *legato* in the performance may make the hunting celebrations sound a little too boozy! Instead, keep the party alive with energetic, vibrant, detached quavers.

Remember that this is a dance, in fact a gavotte, although this one doesn't begin halfway through a bar. To keep it buoyant, shorten the right-hand crotchets and think musically towards bars 2, 4 etc. Finally, don't forget to include lots of dynamic interest to really colour the performance.

A:6 Johann Krieger *Bourrée in A minor*

There are only eight bars to learn in this elegant French dance and, despite the independent left hand in the opening and bar 8, there are few technical difficulties, most of the piece falling comfortably under the fingers. The *legato/staccato* contrast between the hands may take a little persuading into the technique but otherwise the phrasing is matched, effective and worth trying, although of course, not compulsory. Thinking of the fingers as dancers on the keys and choreographing them can enhance the phrasing and help to capture a little more of the character.

The dance really needs a feeling of two-in-a-bar. At the suggested tempo marking (minim = 80) the piece becomes quite lively and buoyant but a slower tempo will also work well, so don't exhaust and confuse the dancers just for the sake of a notch on the metronome.

Listen carefully for unwanted accents on the upbeats, particularly where preceded by a change of hand position or jump, and keep the *staccato* light throughout though not forgetting some dynamic contrast.

B:1 Breslaur *A Romp*

A smooth handover in a relay race might be an enjoyable way of thinking about evenness between the hands. This may be the first time your pupil has met a piece where the melody passes from one hand to the other and matching the tone is obviously important. Gaps between beats two and three each time this crossover happens would spoil the rhythm and the shape of the simple but appealing melody. Try playing the next short phrases at a different dynamic level to show the contrast in the writing. Teachers are sometimes anxious about 'putting in' more dynamics than are printed but imaginative use of tone is always a benefit.

Strong, rhythmic attack gives the middle section a masculine feel in the left hand, while the right hand continues the more feminine patterns as before. Perhaps two sorts of games are happening at the same time here. Thoughtful shaping of the next *ritardando*, *crescendo* and pause will keep the examiner intrigued by these signs of musicality, which mean so much, as will a gentle *ritardando* at the end.

Each time the melody occurs, the fingering should be consistent. These intervals fall easily under small hands and it should be possible to avoid a bump on the first quaver so that 'the romp' begins on the right foot with a clear beat to the first full bar.

A trouble-free piece, suitable for many pupils, providing they can feel the basic beat through the various patterns and can enjoy the different pictures painted by the music.

B:2 C. Gurlitt *Serenade in B flat*

'Some are born great and some have greatness thrust upon them,' Shakespeare remarked. Piano teachers may ruefully think that the same can be said of musicality.

In the small but capable hands of an innately musical pupil, this piece will be a delight. The musical-box effect of the opening develops into a mature and touching harmonic progression which at bars 21 and 22 achieves a lovely falling bass line and deeply expressive treble melody.

Rubato seems a very adult word to apply to a Grade 2 piece but some pupils will automatically respond by elegantly lingering at special moments, then picking up the flowing two-in-a-bar immediately afterwards. Possible places for this are bars 8–9, 15–16, 21–22 and 28 to the end. Beware, though, that if this is overdone it will sound 'taught'and laboured. It must be natural and unaffected.

Left-hand practice is needed for an even flow of quavers and playing chords as preparation for the triad patterns will help the memory latch on to the shapes. The printed fingering is helpful for all sizes of hands and, if the pupil is advanced enough, touches of pedal, twice a bar, will smooth over the quavers and help to create a bar-line-free effect.

Real *cantabile* playing is too much to expect of most Grade 2 candidates but a gentle left-hand accompaniment and a sense of really singing the right-hand melody will go a long way towards creating the right approach. Once again, the ornaments are the icing on the cake and can be left out if they are getting in the way of the essential forward momentum.

Dynamics are mostly gentle, with just the one warmer moment at bar 15, but watch that the tone is not hard here, as these notes are very high on the piano. Phrasing is in four-bar sections, with the main point on the last-but-one beat. Smooth grading towards these points will be needed for real polish. The final line, with its fading tone and last pause, is a gift for the musically sensitive and a chance to savour the silence at the end of this lovely piece, when the music finally fades and the musical box is quietly closed.

B:3 Reinecke *Prelude*

'At last a piece meant for me!' Left-handed pupils often have a hard time with the structure of many early pieces but this one is made for them.

The left-hand melody must carry over the right-hand accompaniment throughout. This is quite a skill and the phrasing is all-important if the piece is to have its proper shape and reflective mood. It will be helpful to mark in separate dynamics for each hand. The printed marks apply to the melody and the right-hand semiquavers should be at a gentler level.

A thoughtful *ritardando* at bar 16, followed by an exact *a tempo*, gives a moment's relaxation before the first melody returns but with a different twist at the end.

Technically, this depends on a very even flow between the hands; a continuous line of semiquavers should sound, with no gaps between left and right hands, or the serenade will have hiccups. Bumping the thumb note of the right-hand patterns needs to be avoided and a relaxed, rolling wrist action here will help to create an even line of sound and avoid any stiffness from the repeated patterns.

Of course, pupils do not have to be left handers to play this piece successfully. A good left-hand *legato* and awareness of forward flow are the starting points. The accents show where a gentle lean will give point to the phrases and, once the notes are safely known, this will be a low-risk piece in terms of accuracy but quite demanding in its musical qualities.

The suggested tempo gives a good sense of direction at which the rising and falling of the dynamics can work smoothly. Too slow a pace will sound laboured but a very brisk performance will lose the essential expressiveness and turn into an efficient but soulless technical exercise.

B:4 Grechaninov *Farewell*

This is the piece for someone who is not a natural reader of the bass clef, being entirely in the treble clef. It does have its disadvantages however. The hands are occasionally fighting for position and it can be a little disconcerting playing with both hands around and above middle C for the duration of the piece. In general, though, it is technically quite straightforward.

This rather sad and tearful farewell will suit the more reflective and imaginative pupil rather than potential Formula 1 racing drivers. The piece needs to be as *espressivo* as possible with a *cantabile*, very *legato* right hand and lots of shape to the phrases. The suggested tempo will help this, giving scope for a natural flexibility and striking an excellent balance between spaciousness and musical direction. Allow the music to breathe between phrases; it needs the space so don't be scared to lift the hands from the keys.

In bars 9, 11 etc take the E with the left hand and don't forget to hold the Gs (bars 10 and 14) as these will warm the harmony. Finally, make the most of the *ritardando* in bar 16 and the *rallentando* at the end as you say your final, unhappy goodbye.

B:5 T. F. Kirchner *Poco Vivace in C*

This is a good-humoured piece and will suit a pupil with a sense of childish fun. Be careful that it doesn't have the last laugh however; it's only *poco vivace* but fingers may well become a little over-eager and run away with a nervous or unsure candidate. To avoid this, take a deep breath before starting, get the hands in position and set the tempo carefully.

There are a lot of quick jumps so watch the hands carefully to check that they move quickly and immediately to the next position, not just to the first note but covering the whole group of notes.

The quick-witted humour continues with a few small rhythmical jokes. After so many semiquavers in the opening bars the counting in bar 5 could catch even the most careful student out so be careful here, and the laughter of the dotted rhythm in the chords needs to be precise (bars 11,17 etc) and mustn't sound too casual. Keep the final two chords of these bars *staccato*, as marked.

Finally, there is an excellent opportunity to experiment with the use of the sustaining pedal here, so do encourage pupils who can reach the pedal to have a go, although it can, of course, be left out by smaller candidates.

B:6 Somervell *Plaintive Waltz*

This attractive waltz haunts the mind long after playing and will richly reward hard work. It soon becomes clear that this was not one of Somervell's happiest holiday memories so to really capture the plaintive mood the gentle, slightly mournful right-hand chords need a light hand/arm, slightly flatter fingers and to be lightly detached. This will prevent them becoming too intrusive and 'beating time' over the left-hand tune.

The left-hand jump from line two to three needs to be handled carefully without taking too much time and avoiding an accent, allowing the right hand to begin its melody uninterrupted. The left-hand accompaniment needs to lightly support the tune, so keep the chords light and allow a little more weight on the bottom notes, perhaps even holding them a little underneath the chords to enhance the harmony.

In order to provide musical direction for the rather lonely notes in bars 14 and 16 and make them seem less exposed, keep them very *legato* and give the line plenty of shape. Enjoy the *ritardando* here, taking a gentle breath before the *a tempo*. Make the most of the final *decrescendo* as the waltz fades into the distance, grading the *ritardando* carefully so that the dance slows gracefully to a close.

C:1 Bartók *Romanian Christmas Carol*

A child listening to this piece will probably hear just a haunting, simple tune, with a repeated catchy rhythm. Adults looking at the printed page will be more aware of the different bar lengths and the possibilities of wrong counting.

The first approach is the safest. When sung as it must have been originally intended, the melody is easy and perhaps lends itself to some words. Why not make up some to suit your pupil? Something like 'Here comes dear old Faaa-ther Christmas' fits the first phrase (even if not in Romanian), and a possibly worrying rhythm suddenly becomes easy. Careful counting will also be important and the 3/8 bars could be thought of in three quavers until the feel of the rhythmic changes takes over.

The notes of each hand are not difficult to play but do check the accidentals carefully, as this is a piece which examiners will sometimes hear with mis-readings. When the hands are put together, they could easily bump into each other in the last line. This is the hardest section to master. Try to keep the left hand quite high and over the top of the right hand, as this is the most helpful way round this corner, and the left hand will see-saw quite comfortably between 5 and 1 on E♭ and D, then E♮ to D♭.

The bar of silence in the middle will probably not be practised at home, except by the most dutiful, and it will be a great temptation to leave it out in the heat of the moment when the exam comes.

Coping with the changes from 2/4 to 3/8 is made easier if pupils concentrate on keeping the 3/8 quavers exactly the same speed as the 2/4 quavers at bars 12–13 and 17–18.

After all this care with counting, it will be a relief to return to the simple idea of an expressive, rather naïve melody, imagined perhaps as sung by children in a snowy Romanian landscape.

C:2 Christopher Norton *Cloudy Day*

This might be a good piece to play first in an exam. The three pieces can be performed in any order and the relaxed atmosphere and few hazards of this one make it a safe bet, which would also settle nerves on the 'Big Day'.

Christopher Norton's pieces and their direct titles always go down well and the candidate's enjoyment will also reach the examiner. That mysterious 'sense of performance' begins to be achievable in many of these approachable jazz miniatures.

Having given that encouragement, the piece still needs some solid musical qualities to make it work. There should be a feel of two-in-a-bar but it is easy to miss the time signature when the four crotchets are so obvious on the page. This is harder to achieve at a slowish tempo, which the piece needs, and *rubato* is also suggested. A groovy feel and natural response to the idiom will be more convincing than trying to apply flexibility by altering note values.

The left-hand chords, especially those at the start that are played without pedal, are tied for a long time, so must have enough warmth to last underneath the melody. Later on, at bar 9, the pedal comes in and its various changes are marked until the end.

There is quite a lot of musical detail. Raindrop *staccato* notes at the start, then *legato* lines with varying dynamics and counting will need a watchful eye at bars 9–12, as the minims could be cut short in the enthusiasm of the *crescendo*.

Examiners will be hoping for all this detail inside a relaxed, slightly sad jazzy framework, which would also benefit from a feel of the improvised effect of the right hand.

C:3 Michael Rose *Cakes and Ale*

The hint of bagpipes in the middle of this rollicking piece suggests we might be at a celebration in Scotland. Cakes and Ale may seem an odd combination to youngsters more used to burgers and coke but the party mood will carry them over such doubts.

The light-footed dance needs a *legato* melody against a *staccato* bass, until the skirl of the pipes in the middle section begins. Plenty of fire on the accents here but keep the rhythm tight. The suggested speed is ideal but a touch either faster or slower will not upset the party, as long as the tempo is consistent and the beat irresistible.

Usually repeats are not played in exams, so the second-time bars can replace bars 7 and 8 to go straight on to bar 9. There is an 'altogether now' feeling when the melody returns at bar 17 and things get really hectic until the bagpipes call a halt.

This is a piece for the nimble-fingered. It needs deft, neat playing in each hand and a really secure basic beat, as well as a sense of fun. Its attractions make up for the challenges and it sounds harder than it actually is, so makes an ideal performance piece for school concerts or when grandma calls for a tune.

C:4 Carol Barratt *Beanery Boogie*

A great hit with young pupils since it was published, this piece is based on a classic 12-bar blues pattern and not only stands as an excellent piece in its own right but could also be the basis for some exciting improvisation practice. Simply get in the groove, oil those fingers and off you go.

Looking ahead is essential as the piece needs to be lively and upbeat. Watch out in particular for those left-hand jumps; they may cause some hesitation, so practise jumping quickly and covering all the next notes in one movement to ensure attention can be directed to the right hand. As a game, you might ask the pupils to jump to the left-hand chord formed by the next few notes a beat early – it's a little tricky but worth the effort. Similarly, encourage the hand to begin stretching early for the right-hand octave in bar 12.

The right-hand fingering is consistent throughout and makes the playing of the blues scale extremely easy, although some pupils may find 1-2-1 in bar 10 a little unfamiliar, if extremely sensible.

A lively, brisk tempo and plenty of dynamic contrast will be the tomato sauce on the beans and a courageous leap and good *fortissimo* tone on the final Cs will add that extra 'je ne sais quoi'.

C:5 Kabalevsky *Nights on the River*

This evocative piece conjures up strong images of a gently flowing river and the static left hand portrays the reflection on the surface. Use as much imaginative teaching language as possible to encourage a beautiful shape to the right-hand line, an unobtrusive left hand and an immaculate *legato*. A dab or two of pedal will warm the harmonies if the pupil can cope (and reach) but don't use it to hold the bass notes. These must be held down with the fingers for their full length to allow the pedal freedom to change (if used), enhance the harmony and so give the river its depth.

Some of the fingering can be adjusted but it is well-thought-out to achieve a seamless *legato*, even if quite a lot of flexibility is needed in the fingers and hand to achieve this in bar 10. Listen to the ends of phrases and, if gently separating them, match the left hand to the right hand where marked. Remember that a controlled *pianissimo* is needed at the end and nervous fingers may well fail to produce a tone if it is too tentative, so encourage a warm *piano* in the opening to give scope for the final *diminuendo*.

C:6 Jerzy Lefeld *Little Mouse*

Not only does this piece sound like the scampering and squeaking of a mouse but also the grace notes and quavers somehow look like paw prints.

Pupils may be a little confused by the layout of this little character piece but the notes are not hard. The main problem will be some unease due to the fingers being almost constantly above the keys except for the semiquavers; nervous hands may stray or get a little disorientated. Its title will appeal, however, and it is an excellent choice for small hands and a cheeky personality.

Making the hand shape look like a 'mouse hole' for the semiquaver runs will have added meaning here and, together with a light hand, will help ensure that the mouse scampers easily and evenly up and down the semiquavers. Put in the grace notes straight away, playing them together with the main note to begin with, then articulating the notes slightly. All the jumps need to be prepared at the very first opportunity to allow sufficient fluency, so a lot of 'shadow jumping' may help.

Finally, take note of the dynamic markings and phrasing and don't forget the change of clef in the final bar as the mouse disappears into its hole.

GRADE 3

Pupils should be well into their stride by now and will probably have stronger views on the choice of their programme. The Basis of Assessment shows the same requirements for Pass, Merit and Distinction for Grades 1–5, but with the understanding that these elements will be progressively developed through the grades. Different tone colours should be emerging by now, as well as a more confident response to the different styles.

LIST A
The Rameau is likely to be the safest choice for the technically cautious. The 'Anglaise in D minor' and Bach 'Allegro in G' both need good keyboard geography and facility, while the other C. P. E. Bach item, the 'Menuet: La Pott', has some subtle detail. The Handel 'Bourrée' is bright and breezy, providing the few dangerous corners are reliably under control.

LIST B
Balance between the hands becomes an important issue in several pieces. The Burgmüller, Diabelli and Tchaikovsky all need this awareness and deserve expressive phrasing to do justice to their lovely melodies. The 'Little Flower' is wonderful in musical hands, as is the Hofmann 'Melody', and the Kirchner 'Vivace in F' is ideal for those with more vitality and rhythm than lyrical qualities.

LIST C
The two jazzy items, 'Blues in Two' and 'There ain't no beer in Cow-Horn Creek!', need a natural affinity with the style and the Cornick will benefit from some pedal. The Stravinsky is not too demanding technically and will suit imaginative pupils, as will the Bartók. The Finnissy is quite sophisticated and the Kodály needs plenty of bravura.

A:1 Anon. *Anglaise in D minor*

I wonder if you, like me, feel that this composer had a rather rustic view of the English. There is a definite agricultural and 'mud-filled boots' character to this anglaise and I suspect the composer may have been too embarrassed to attach his name securely to this composition in case he'd offended. It is a strong and attractive dance, however, with plenty of rhythmic energy, so don't miss the opportunity to show the parallels between this and some popular music. A sort of 18th-century rock 'n' roll.

The secret to keeping the dance's buoyancy will be to employ a vibrant tempo (minim = 84 is a good suggestion) and to detach the left-hand crotchets. They should not be too short though; make them a little more robust. Articulate the opening left-hand quavers well, separating the right-hand minims, and don't be scared to throw the accent onto the second beat in bars 4, 8 and similar bars for that stamp of the feet.

The editorial phrasing needs to be considered carefully. There is a danger that it will create a semiquaver–dotted quaver rhythm and an unwanted accent on beats 2 and 4, whereas one of the features of an anglaise is, in fact, a strong first beat. If problems occur, try phrasing the crotchet with the following quavers.

All right-hand quavers need to be even and ornaments to be kept light if the fingers are to be allowed the freedom to move quickly enough. Don't forget to practise the *dal segno*, particularly the left-hand jump, which is a classic moment for exam hesitation.

Finally, enjoy experimenting with the dynamics. There is no right solution but some very effective possibilities, particularly in creating a contrasting middle section (bars 13–20). Be sure to finish with aplomb.

A:2 C. P. E. Bach *Allegro in G*

This humorous allegro is a terrific piece for budding long-jumpers. Be careful, though – it isn't quite as macho as it may seem, because the musical athlete then has to worry about the subtlety of his or her landing.

C. P. E. Bach was the second son of J. S. Bach and the leading keyboard teacher of his time. In this energetic and sprightly piece he has clearly set out to test both his pupils' fearless leaps and instinct for tone. At the same time, however, the musical rewards for all this training are enormous and well worth the effort.

The piece will rely on effective phrasing and a bright cheerful tone for a lively and charismatic performance. Keep the upbeat quavers detached and light and the semiquavers evenly articulated. Bars 4, 6, 8 etc will need attention as the hands will be travelling fast to their new destination and an uncontrolled leap could result in an unwanted accent. Instead, practise the jump slowly, covering the note and then preparing the sound and articulation until it becomes second nature.

Remind the pupils of the changes of clef before they begin learning the notes. How many times have teachers had to undo a whole week's well-intentioned practice because of such a misreading?

The suggested dynamics and tempo will add to the excitement and, together with technical fluency, enable a performance that will be a hit not just in the exam but at any end-of-term concert.

A:3 Rameau *Menuet in A minor*

This is a charming and very beautiful piece. Rameau was (so the story goes) thrown out of school at the age of seven because he could read any piece of harpsichord music but nothing else. I wonder whether this explains why this piece can't quite make up its mind whether it is an aria or a menuet.

Hidden melodies abound in the lower notes of the right hand. Use the suggested phrasing to enhance these but don't take them too literally. Shortening the second quaver of each couplet too abruptly will give the dancers hiccups.

This menuet is technically fairly straightforward – just an elegant glide along the keyboard, keeping the left-hand crotchets gently detached. If this proves difficult, then the piece works well with the left-hand *legato* or at a slightly more moderate tempo. Don't allow the ornaments to become too panicked or abrupt; treat them all melodically and end each phrase gracefully.

The block dynamics provide a useful starting point for musical interest, akin to using different stops on a two-manual harpsichord, but bear in mind that harpsichordists use various techniques for further expressiveness inappropriate to the piano. Instead, try out the occasional *crescendo* or *diminuendo* and allow a full range of shape to each phrase. You might, for instance, consider a *piano* in bar 5 and a *crescendo* to bar 8.

There is plenty of grace, unhurried elegance, colour and charm to explore here; it is a real treat to play.

A:4 C. P. E. Bach *Menuet: La Pott*

There are some mysteries to be solved here. Apart from its intriguing title, there is very little in the way of musical signposts: no tempo indication, no dynamics, just some slurs and appoggiaturas. Did he really intend a B♭ at bars 2 and 10, we wonder?

One mystery at least can be solved. Herr Johann Heinrich Pott was a theologian, doctor and chemist but presumably still had time to dance the occasional menuet. C. P. E. Bach wrote a series of these pieces dedicated to his friends in Berlin.

The stately dance, with its characteristic strong first beat in each bar, gives the foundation and ensures that the triplet sub-divisions fall evenly within the three beats. Possible problems here might be laboured triplets slowing the pulse, or uneven quavers sounding more like two semiquavers and a quaver.

The opening phrase extends, despite sub-divisions, as far as bar 8 and, although no dynamics are marked, it will be so much more interesting to hear some contrast. A gentle start at bar 9, building to the end of the first section, would work well and similar ideas are possible, as you choose. Pupils will be pleased to be asked which dynamics they would like to play and a performance is usually much more convincing if pupils believe that it is their own interpretation they are communicating.

The slurs help to give the graceful lean and lift of the period and you may like to add more in pairs at bars 22–23, 27 and 29–30. The trill in bar 31 could be reduced to a simple mordent, starting on the beat, which is less risky than a longer ornament.

The melody line lies on top of the right-hand chords, so the lower notes need to be gentle. This is not easy when the thumb is playing many of them but keeping the weight towards the outside of the hand will help.

Rests are an important part of the rhythm. Encourage pupils to 'pick their feet up' exactly on time and perhaps detach the left-hand crotchets, if you like the effect. The pause at bar 16 is for the end of the *da capo* only, not a breathing space in the middle of the piece.

It makes a welcome change to have scope for your own ideas in performance and this is particularly enjoyable in such a traditional-sounding piece. Perhaps C. P. E. Bach was gently poking fun at one of his distinguished friends, but Herr Pott would no doubt be flattered to know that 'his' menuet is still being played all these years later.

A:5 Handel *Bourrée*

This sounds like bright and breezy flute music and so it is. Examiners will recognize this piece as part of the flute syllabus from a few years back. They will also remember the slightly anxious anticipation of the quaver runs at bars 5–8 and bar 15 to the end, which sometimes came adrift, causing that well-worn comment, 'After a promising start . . .'.

Most of this is technically straightforward but pianists may have similar problems to those of the flautists unless the fingering is settled early in the learning process and can be relied on in the heat of the moment.

Youngsters often enjoy playing 'those bars' in isolation then having a quick dash around the room before playing them again to see if they are still safe.

Fingering is such a personal matter. Size of hands, a preference for certain approaches and several other factors all play a part but, in this kind of piece, early planning of fingering is wise. The printed suggestions will suit most hands but are not the only solution for the quavers. Whatever the decision, the fingers need to be consistent at each playing, so that the tempo can be confidently maintained.

As this is another early dance, a light-hearted, rhythmic approach, with a sprightly tempo will catch the mood. The small but significant *staccato* sign at the start applies to the bass crotchets and will also help to give zest to the playing.

The suggested dynamics are well worth trying but a quiet moment in E minor would add colour to bars 11–12. The beginning of the long *crescendo* is best played really quietly each time, so that the tone doesn't build too quickly and over-blow the climax.

Young – and not so young – often tend to hurry during a *crescendo*, especially when playing quavers. Keeping firmly in touch with the basic beat will prevent that dangerous 'leaning forward' effect, which will unsettle players and listeners alike.

The final two bars can be comfortably negotiated with a small *ritardando* and this also helps the last chord to arrive on cue, with all four notes safely assembled.

A:6 Telemann *Très Vite*

This is a rare item in an exam list – a piece with no fewer than fifteen commas in the score. The ones in brackets have been added for consistency of approach. So what should be the approach?

Trying to add this punctuation by creating tiny breaks would disrupt the rhythm and is not what is intended. All that is needed is a fresh start every other bar. The commas simply remind us that fingers in each hand should be lifted, so that no overlap across the bar line spoils the clean articulation.

Despite the E minor key, the clean texture of this piece is lively and invigorating, especially if managed at a brisk tempo. The right feel will be achieved by a two-in-a-bar beat, which is hinted at by the minim metronome mark. The latter may be on the optimistic side at 108 but the piece could succeed at a slower speed, provided that the rhythm has vitality and that the weaker crotchets in each bar are lighter than the first beats.

Pupils will soon spot the bonus of relatively few notes to learn, as there is quite a lot of repetition. Finding a different way of expressing the same phrases needs some imagery that will strike a bell in young minds. The potential tedium of repeating words in the same tone of voice can be easily demonstrated. Pupils enjoy finding a different way to say the same sentence and then transferring the idea into the music. Putting 'modern', everyday words to the opening phrase can have the effect of crossing the centuries and making an ancient melody much more approachable. Something like, 'Come in James, have a cup of tea', goes a long way to dispelling the 'exam piece' syndrome.

There is plenty of work for each hand to ensure safe independence and consistent fingering. The two parts are beautifully balanced in terms of activity, so the line that is busiest always comes over easily.

Some of the detail, such as slurs over just two quavers and the trill at bar 4, may be too ambitious for all except the very deft but, if they are included, also add them in the corresponding places later.

The dynamics work in strongly contrasted sections, with an open choice as to which level to play the final four bars. Whether you choose a quiet or more positive ending, the last couple of bars should leave the listener in no doubt that this is in fact the end.

B:1 J. F. F. Burgmüller *Innocence*

This is one of the many delightful, tuneful studies for young pianists by Johann Burgmüller. If you haven't already explored them then do. Pupils today still enjoy their youthful energy and charm.

This is a rather deceptive title since technically the piece is anything but innocent. I suspect Burgmüller is looking down on us with something of a smile and a 'what, me?' expression on his face. Those pupils who have experienced running down a grassy hill, finding themselves out of control and eventually landing in an ungainly heap at the bottom, will immediately recognize the dangers behind those descending semiquavers. On the other hand, the *character* of this piece is all about elegance, charm and innocence and to express this the runs need to be well controlled and unflustered.

Try hearing the first notes of each group of semiquavers as the melody; pupils might even practise playing just these and listening to the triads they form. They should then sense a slower melody behind the notes and this will help the control. Charm the listener with the little 'curtseys' in the music (bars 2, 4 etc). These written-out appoggiaturas all need a little more warmth of tone on the first note and a light second note.

The left hand is (thankfully) much easier than the right but don't neglect it. Shape the chords with the right-hand melody where appropriate and keep the left hand smooth, even and light under the skipping right hand from bar 9. Generally, keep the whole piece light and smiling with a cheeky grin at the end.

B:2 Diabelli *Andante*

The editorial comment provides the teacher with a wonderful opportunity to indulge in some listening at the beginning of the lesson. A performance of the waltz theme provided to Beethoven and the first few variations will help put this piece into some context amidst the knowledge that Diabelli also published some of Beethoven's works. You might also play through the other two movements of the Sonatina.

This is a warm, richly expressive piece and will suit a pupil with a natural breadth; singers, in particular, will relate to the phrasing and recognize those moments when a little time is required for a breath. If the piece still sounds a little hurried and shapeless, try putting some words to the phrases; anything will do, however silly. Try, for instance, 'I always go to see my Gran and Grandad on a Saturday' for the second phrase; the use of one syllable for each semiquaver will help give them direction and spaciousness.

The left hand needs to be unobtrusive yet supportive. Perhaps think of the sort of sound a small string orchestra might make, using short bow strokes for the quaver chords.

Interpret the wedges within an early 19th-century context – merely a normal and unaccented *staccato* – and treat the dynamics with respect, although a little interpretation is needed in bars 4–5, where an abrupt *mezzo forte* would sound a little contrived. I suspect Diabelli was merely encouraging the performer to remember to sing out the melody.

Technically, the piece is fairly straightforward. Make sure hands prepare the beginnings of phrases carefully to avoid an accent, phrase the chords in bar 18 with a relaxed and giving wrist and enjoy the final pause, which provides welcome space and time to breathe and relax.

B:3 Tchaikovsky *Old French Song*

A French song, written by a Russian and in all probability performed by a pupil who is of yet another nationality. This actually fits in quite well with Tchaikovsky's own life, since he travelled abroad quite widely.

As with all songs, this piece needs a *cantabile* tone and a good balance will be crucial, keeping the accompaniment gentle and unobtrusive. The shape and breathing within the melody will always be best encouraged if the pupil can put some words to the music. No cheating though; they really should be French words (with a Russian accent!).

Listen carefully to the upbeat; there will be a tendency to place an emphasis here, so the hand needs to be kept light. The phrasing in bar 8 is a little curious. The D is marked as the end of the previous phrase but every instinct says that it should be the beginning of the next (as suggested by the *pianissimo* marking).

There can be little doubt that the piece is in G minor, with all those bottom Gs in the left hand. They need to be held down quite conscientiously to provide the harmonic support, with careful note taken as to which ones are tied. Do avoid accenting them, though, as they mustn't intrude on the melody. The middle section (bars 17–24) is a contrast to the seamless opening, though the left-hand *staccato* should not be too short; think of the notes as a gentle *pizzicato* or the padding paw-prints of a pet cat or dog.

There is no pedal marked in the piece but if your pupil instinctively uses some then encourage this. It will need to be fairly subtle, though, to avoid too many blurred harmonies. There is an excellent opportunity for adding some pedal in the final two bars, however.

The dynamics are generally quiet but many an examiner has heard valiant attempts at *pianissimo* go sadly wrong on an unfamiliar piano and with the tentativeness of exam nerves. Avoid starting too softly, upgrade each dynamic one level – and why not use the *una corda* in bars 8 to 16 to provide a different colour?

B:4 C. Gurlitt *Little Flower*

First choose your flower. We know that the small wild *mignonette* was probably in Gurlitt's mind when he wrote this affectionate little piece. Any simple garden flower, known to your pupil, will help to conjure up the right tone-colour and mood.

Cantabile playing, with its singing tone and use of arm weight, is rare at this level but examiners will notice with delight if the beginnings of this skill are showing in some passages. The opening interval of a sixth is a good chance to lean on the top G but gently does it, as the phrase is marked *piano* and *dolce*. The left hand also has a similar opportunity in bars 14–15 when it crosses over the right hand.

It's quite easy to use weight on the thumb or fifth fingers to achieve this carrying tone but more advanced to apply this technique to the other fingers. Some pupils learn this knack quite quickly and, ideally, all the melody notes should have this singing tone.

The phrasing is not very obvious to the eye but more so to the ear. A gentle emphasis on the feminine endings, for example the G at the end of the first four-bar phrase, will give the shape which conveys the graceful, wistful mood.

Possible traps lie in the rhythm of the middle section, from bar 9–14. It would be all too tempting to start the left-hand octaves too soon after the crotchet rests. Pupils will need to listen carefully to the tone in each hand here, so that there is a really smooth *crescendo*, peaking as the left hand takes over at bars 14 and 15. The pedal is marked at this point which will help the effect. Sensitive shaping of the *ritardando* going to bar 16 is part of the charm of the style, so try to find just the right moment to restart the main melody at the *a tempo*.

The left hand will need warm, lasting sounds to support the main theme and, if your pupil is confident with the pedal, either *legato* pedalling, changing twice in each bar, or touches of direct pedalling on the main beats, will help the colour and enhance the *legato*.

The suggested tempo of *andantino* is ideal. Any slower and the piece could become too sad and ponderous for this miniature but too fast a speed would sound matter-of-fact and uncaring.

TLC – tender loving care – is an expression which your pupils will know and this piece will reward those who can lavish this kind of sensitivity on its preparation and performance.

B:5 H. Hofmann *Melody*

What has a travelling walkway at an airport got to do with this piece? Potentially, quite a lot. The smooth, inevitable forward flow, which pupils may have experienced when going to the departure gate, is tremendously helpful in getting them to relate this progression to musical phrasing. These *legato*, romantic lines need to flow gently forwards and always travel evenly. The left-hand quavers add to this effect, once the mental imagery is in place.

Hofmann's choirboy youth shows in this very vocal melody. Humming along, an octave down where necessary, will create the right *legato* feel and make the fingers want to join the sounds into seamless lines.

Two kinds of technique will help to lift the playing beyond the rather mundane, pedestrian approach that is sometimes heard in this style.

Let's consider the left hand first. A gentle rocking action between the quavers will keep an even background and prevent any stiffness as the patterns flow onwards. The rising and falling of the melody is enhanced by a flexible, balancing accompaniment. So often examiners hear a potentially graceful right-hand melody obscured by a prominent, uniform level beneath.

Bar 7 is the one to tackle first. Lots of slow practice, with the top line as connected as possible, will avoid any sudden loss of tempo which may threaten this corner and also bar 15, to a lesser extent.

A *legato*, *cantabile* tone in the right hand is ideally needed. Aiming for this special tone quality on the longer notes to begin with, and particularly at main points of phrases (such as the first beat of bar 4), is a good basis for future development.

The musical details, *crescendi*, *diminuendi*, dynamics, *poco ritardando* and *a tempo*, are both individually important and contribute to the warmly expressive mood. The final three bars gently fade away with the help of some *legato* pedalling, which is marked. Make the most of the final pause and release the fingers and the foot together.

A happy melody, this one, with elements of sensitive, skilful piano playing which will last a lifetime of music-making, if instilled with awareness at this stage.

B:6 T. F. Kirchner *Vivace in F*

Vitality is infectious. Candidates who burst into the exam room and can't wait to begin are endearing, but examiners will also expect that a tendency to rush might need a gentle restraining hand during lessons.

The two contrasted ideas here need both a sense of immediacy and of fun, with the underlying pulse keeping the rhythm secure. Quite a brisk tempo is indicated and, once under the fingers, the notes are comfortably despatched at an invigorating pace, providing that the basic beat is still felt.

Impeccably even semiquavers and *staccato* notes, all of exactly the same length, are more the province of orchestral players. Pianists of all ages find this degree of precision difficult. Perhaps imagining that a trumpet is playing the first two bars, then flutes the light answering phrase, may help to get to grips with this sort of clarity and control.

Fingering suggestions are sensible here, particularly the 2-1 decoration on each descending quaver. You need to be as quick as a blink on these, with the right-hand chords even lighter.

Bars 9–12 provide a bit more drama with some heroic, but not too strident, octaves at bar 10, followed by a small *ritardando*. Conductors would make sure the spaces between the notes in bar 12 were gradually increased in a predictable way and examiners would love to hear this kind of care given to a seemingly small moment.

In an excess of enthusiasm, pupils sometimes lift their hands high off the keys in *staccato* passages. Once the key has returned to its resting position, it makes no difference at all whether the hands are half an inch or two feet above. Keeping close to the keys is much the safest approach and the descending quavers and chords are probably safest played while looking at the keyboard.

The two-in-a-bar time signature is rather like the regular stride of a marching band. This, and the contrasted instruments idea, should evoke a military mood of controlled stability, rather than the understandable, but dangerous, 'Charge of the Light Brigade' approach!

C:1 Mike Cornick *Blues in Two*

What pupil will not be tempted by this smoochy yet melancholy number and what an excellent opportunity to explore some jazz blues on CD: some Ray Charles or Louis Jordan, or even recorded excerpts in the CD ROM encyclopaedias that many children now have access to.

Notice that this piece is in swing rhythm so there are no equal quavers. If a pupil is unfamiliar with this, then practise some scales in swing rhythm or try tapping triplet rhythms with the hands whilst marking the beat with the feet. If the opening rhythm still proves elusive then ignore the ties, playing the C twice.

It will be difficult not to notice the flattened 3rd 'blue' note (A♭ in the opening, D♭ later on) as it forms the focus to each phrase. You might perhaps use this opportunity to discuss the blues scale and even to begin an improvisation session using the blues scale over some of the left-hand harmonies.

The piece needs a warm, rich tone and real *legato* line. Imagine an alto saxophone playing the melody, or better still try to find a pupil or friend who could play it or record it. The tone will be helped by pedal, which will need to change on, but not before, each bass note (except in bars 14 and 15, where it will need to change each beat). Allow a little more tone on the bass notes than on the chords but in general keep the right hand singing and to the fore.

If you really want to give the piece an improvisatory feel then you might like to encourage the pupil to learn it from memory. It can be played 'from memory with the music' in the exam and would allow a characteristic and much-needed freedom and spontaneity.

C:2 Kodály *Children's Dance*

Those budding virtuosi amongst your pupils will love this lively and energetic Hungarian dance but must first take off their ballet shoes. It needs plenty of bravura, confidence and a robust sense of rhythm.

The piece is actually a theme and two variations: the eight-bar right-hand melody is played three times, each time with a different character. The first might be the ladies, dancing with exuberance but also with charm, the second the children and the third the men with their heavy boots.

The more astute amongst your pupils will notice a slightly Chinese tinge to the piece. The melody is in fact a pentatonic scale and provides an opportunity to link in various other pieces, particularly some Scottish tunes, many of the finest of which are based on this scale.

The suggested fingering throughout the piece is a little unusual but don't dismiss it – it works extremely well and avoids a jumping hand. Notice the *staccato/legato* contrast in the opening and give the left-hand crotchet nearly its full length, coming off with the right hand except in bar 4. This left-hand crotchet may also cause a little confusion in bars 5 to 8. Notice how it changes and choose a suitable fingering to ensure the hand knows where it is going.

Observe the dynamics and keep something in reserve for the *fortissimo* towards the end. Be careful not to get too carried away with the left-hand chords here – we still need to hear the right-hand melody.

The final *piano* chord finishes the piece rather cheekily. The ending will work better without a *ritenuto*; instead, 'place' the final chord just slightly and hold for at least three beats.

C:3 Stravinsky *Larghetto*

Yet another piece for the reluctant bass-clef reader from a noted ballet composer and excellent writer of simple children's pieces.This is a slow, haunting and melancholy dance and needs a colourful, choreographed image in the performer's mind to capture the rather strange phrase lengths and charm.

Notice that the first phrase is just three notes long and that subsequent phrases build in length, together forming one large phrase of six bars, which gives the piece a timeless quality. The gentle lilting rhythm is only disturbed twice for a little trumpet fanfare (bars 10 and 12), which perhaps announces the arrival of the King or Queen to the dance.

The right hand falls very kindly under five fingers, as the volume this piece is taken from (*Les Cinq Doigts*) suggests. The left-hand part is not so considerate but, nonetheless, there are no obvious problems for the pupil. Instead, there are some rather subtle moments of technical difficulty to overcome, particularly some 'finger-fun' holding the dotted crotchets in the second section of the piece and carefully grading Stravinsky's own dynamics.

The opening hasn't been given a dynamic by the composer, so experiment; ask the pupil to explore his or her own ideas and see where it leads.

There is scope for a little subtle pedal in the piece if the pupil is experienced enough. It does add another dimension and is worth trying although, of course, it also works without.

Keep the final few bars a little lighter, particularly the left-hand chords, although there is no need to bring out the lower right-hand part, you'll be relieved to know. This will be heard anyway as it is the only moving part. A slightly understated end works well here, with hardly any *ritenuto* and exactly six quaver beats on the final chord.

C:4 Bartók *Peasant's Flute*

Perhaps Bartók happened to hear a peasant improvising a haunting tune. It's difficult to transfer the simple freedom of this melody onto the page and Bartók has given us plenty of instructions for recreating his ideas.

There is an almost bewildering array of markings, so let's look first at the basics and consider the detail later. The melody is played twice, lasting eight bars each time, with the two final bars added for an echo effect, which dies completely away.

As we might expect in a peasant's world, exact time is not a priority. The three-in-a-bar melody has a flexible feel, sometimes with a lingering third beat, but underneath this improvised freedom there is a regular steadying pulse, which prevents the piece wandering aimlessly along. The left-hand chords that fill in the gaps on the third beat would be all too easy to put down early and care must be paid to ensure that they are not played straight after the right hand, a quaver too soon.

A relaxed walking tempo catches the atmosphere and the composer's detailed musical markings leave us in no doubt about how to shape the melody. He gently warns us to keep the semiquavers at bar 5 tranquil. When this figure reappears at bar 13, the left-hand chord coincides with the right-hand D – not as complicated as it looks. Some early counting in quavers will protect pupils against wrongly learned rhythms, which are so hard to correct later.

This is outdoors music and the phrases seem to fade, as if heard from a distance. The chords suggest a drone type of accompaniment. Perhaps a friend joins in for the walk and plays to accompany the flute.

The tone quality needs a carrying clarity, without harshness, and a careful judgement of dynamic levels. Playing too quiet too soon would make the left-hand chords stick out at bar ends. Aim to match the sounds between hands in these places, as the melody always predominates, with the chords providing a little harmonic flavour.

The final bars are an ideal chance to hold the atmosphere. If the final E were to fail to sound, there would still be time to play it again and the examiner would admire the candidate's presence of mind.

C:5 Michael Finnissy *No. 4 from 'Wee saw footprints'*

'Wee saw footprints'. . . . It's good to have this clue from the composer and the 'Scottish snap' rhythm of the semiquaver–dotted quaver adds conviction to the highland mood. This is obviously a brisk outdoor walk at around crotchet = 132, probably to avoid the cold – footprints in the snow?

Teachers will immediately have two concerns. First, the rhythm of the melody and then how *legato* to make each line. There are some largish intervals to cover in each hand.

The rhythmic problems disappear with the help of a regular crotchet beat. Some vertical pencil lines drawn through beats two and three will give clear visual guidance as to what group of notes fits into which time span. Being aware of the next main beat prevents the triplets taking up too much time. The sub-divisions are not as complex as they look on the page and are more to do with a feel for this Scottish melody and its national rhythms rather than a mathematical exactitude. The main crotchet beat holds the whole piece together and this can't be compromised.

Left-hand practice in tempo will also help to make decisions about fingering. It's often not until the piece has been learnt to some extent that final decisions about which finger to use can be made. An unbroken *legato* is unlikely here but the crotchets should have even, exact lengths and be phrased to complement the four-bar melody sections. A combination of common sense and thinking ahead to the next leap will help in these decisions.

Similar choices exist in the right-hand melody. Unless pedal is used throughout, which is not required at this stage, a perfect *legato* will be a challenge and is not really implied by the various slurs and accents. Despite its simple appearance on the page and lack of printed dynamic variety, the melody has its own natural rise and fall. Almost a tune to whistle – it might be an ideal aural test for a spot-check on clapping or singing back a phrase, especially when the piece is new to your pupil.

A bracing rhythm, even, walking crotchets and confident covering of the intervals, go a long way towards a successful performance, even if haggis is not your favourite food.

C:6 Pamela Wedgwood *There ain't no beer in Cow-Horn Creek!*

Adult candidates will fall on this one with glee, as will many young players. It's easy to be confident with the style of the music if it's already familiar from TV Westerns, so there will be enthusiasm from the start.

Possible danger areas to consider are the rhythm at bar 13 (not too early with the right-hand chord on the second beat) and the B♭ on the last beat of bar 6. Be sure to play the B♮ on the first beat of bar 11.

Lazy, hot afternoon music can sound boring, so phrasing will be important to give shape and purpose to the ambling gait. The 'sober beat' suggestion of dotted crotchet = *c.*72–80 is just right for the tired horse's walk. Faster would be much too energetic.

Go for a really smooth *legato* in each hand, noticing that the accents are for emphasis, not dramatic stabs. The bass line also needs firmly held minims beneath the well-known cowboy crotchet–quaver rhythm, which obviously continues at the same pace throughout the piece.

44

Some well-judged rises and falls in dynamics add character and, after the *crescendo* to the accented bars 4 and 5, the tone continues warmly to bar 8. Make the most of the quieter moment at bars 11–12 before the last *forte* right-hand sixth. More than a hint of irritation seems to be creeping in at this point, as the lack of a saloon in Cow-Horn Creek strikes home.

The final three bars need careful planning of tone and there's a feeling of a resigned sigh with the 'no beer' last notes. It will be fun to see if any candidates will say the words out loud. Perhaps this is best left for the brave, or for those carried away by a really authentic Western performance.

GRADE 4

Although it is possible to use the pedal from Grade 1 (providing children can reach it), most pupils begin to use the sustaining pedal on a regular basis by this grade. The two forms, direct and *legato* pedalling, both potentially feature in these lists, particularly in List B, which continues to have the more warmly expressive pieces. Grade 4 is generally thought of as the last of the 'baby grades', after which technical capability and musical awareness are rather more integrated.

LIST A
The Clementi will be a favourite and both the Cimarosa and the anonymous 'March in E flat' are easier than the Bach, which will nevertheless appeal to those who will love it for its quality and pedigree. The Handel and Attwood are both very attractive but need good control and technical confidence.

LIST B
Some experience of pedalling will particularly help the Schumann and the Granados, which, with the Gurlitt, are the most immediately attractive choices. The Glière needs a measure of musical maturity and the 'Dance of the Elves' is right for confident players, good at brave leaps – not one for the nervous but fun to learn. The Heller study is a challenge but could be easily the favourite for potential virtuosi of the future.

LIST C
There are some terrific contrasts of style here and identification with the mood of the piece eventually chosen is even more vital than before. 'Sad Story' stands alone in its atmosphere but 'Baa, Baa, Blue Sheep's Waltz' would also suit the pensively inclined. 'Burlesque' and 'Jeering Song' are the extroverted technical show pieces and the jazzy choices are 'You and Me' and 'Laid-back Blues'; the former is the slightly more straightforward of the two.

A:1 J. S. Bach *Menuet*

A domestic exchange in a minor key? We know that Bach wrote this menuet for his wife, Anna Magdalena, and the two parts each have something to say, but the treble line scarcely gives the bass a chance to get a word in edgeways. Only when the right hand pauses on a dotted minim does the left hand manage to fill the space with some eloquent quavers.

On the practical rather than the imaginative side, the right-hand quavers need secure fluency, which will only be reliable with planned fingering and lots of practice, a few bars at a time. 'Less is more' in the preparation of this kind of piece and a couple of bars thoroughly played into the fingers are much more productive in the long term than a whole section hurried through just before the lesson.

The dynamics are editorial but help to show where the dialogue takes a different turn. Almost more important than these suggestions of variety is the phrasing of the quaver patterns which, although having its own conversational spontaneity, always needs to have a main point. The first phrase tends to peak on the first beat of bar 7 and similar patterns can be found in the last couple of bars of each main phrase.

The various slurs and small phrase marks are only suggestions and may be too much to ask of pupils who are finding plenty to grapple with in the weaving quavers.

Left-hand crotchets add a dainty dance step if slightly detached but can also be *legato*, if preferred. Either way, the first beat needs more vitality than beats two and three. Three equally weighted crotchets make for a stodgy bass line, but with all this action in the right hand, a good level of finger security needs to be reached before these refinements can be a practical possibility.

The conversation does not need to be repeated; just play the second-time bars then go on to the end, where the two voices finally resolve on a welcome octave.

A:2 Cimarosa *Sonata in G*

At first glance, this looks a much easier option than the Bach. Cimarosa cheerfully states the obvious with the opening few bars but the crunch comes with the G minor middle section, where the right hand has some demanding thirds. 'Loss of tempo at points of difficulty', is a typical comment from an examiner on a mark form, where a promising start has given way to obstacles 'en route'.

A buoyant tempo, one-in-a-bar, will avoid any pedestrian boredom and really clear tonal contrasts will give the start of each section a fresh impact.

Hidden in the middle of a textbook-style teaching piece are some chances for unconventional but eminently practical fingerings. In the right hand in bar 12, try using the thumb on the C♯ – much easier than the stretch from 2nd to 4th for most smaller hands. Bar 27 can be fingered more comfortably by starting on the 3rd and then using the thumb again on the F♯. Yes, it's quite acceptable to do this, so the whole group is 3/1, 2/1, 3/1, 4/2, 5/3 and much easier to control. There is a final chance to defy the fingering conventions by putting the thumb on the F♯ in bar 41.

There is an opportunity to show real phrasing in the bass-line quavers; it is so much more interesting to rise and fall with the right-hand lines, rather than chugging along at the all-purpose *mezzo forte* that left hands are prone to adopt.

The repeated notes naturally detach themselves and this could continue throughout, but with rising scale passages such as in bars 17–20, possibly more *legato* for a change, if you like the effect. The single mordent in bar 30 looks rather lonely but is worth adding deftly on the beat, unless it upsets the rhythm, in which case leave it out.

Above all, be bold with the overall approach.

A:3 Clementi *Allegretto*

Teachers will recognize this with nostalgia, many having played it themselves in their own youth. Standards of pieces certainly stay the same and this old favourite has appeared for many years in the Grade 4 lists. The bright, jaunty melody stays as fresh as ever and the semiquaver runs will reward those who regularly incorporate scales and finger exercises into their practice sessions.

Musical detail is sometimes added after the notes have been learnt but this 'icing the cake' method is not ideal, though better than no awareness of the markings at all. Much more successful is an approach that includes the phrasing and dynamic levels from the start. The hundreds of subtle physical responses needed are then programmed in with the notes and become a natural part of the whole.

Classical phrasing often depends on just a gentle lean on a note that looks quite insignificant on the page. The feminine endings, the first on the

B at bar 4, contrast with straightforward ends such as at bar 22. It is well worth going on a 'spot the phrase point' mission with pupils, who will then learn to look for themselves where phrases reach their peak.

A jaunty tempo and lots of dynamic contrast give the necessary vitality but beware of overenthusiastic accents marked *sforzando*; these are only to show the change of harmony beneath. Balance of hands will be an important factor – knowing when the left hand should accompany discreetly and when it should make a more positive point, such as the ascending scale passages.

This old friend will be given a warm welcome back and introduced to a new generation of young pianists. No doubt Clementi would be delighted, as he had a particular affection for the young.

A:4 Anon. *March in E flat*

Yet another excellent piece from the *Anna Magdalena Bach Book* and if your pupil has managed to avoid triplets so far then this is a very good introduction. A march is played to encourage orderly marching and take the mind off any tiredness; it needs a firm pulse, with the characteristic drum beat at the back of one's mind.

There is no recommended tempo marking but it is worth noting that an army generally marches at a speed of 75 or 108 steps a minute, depending on whether it is a slow or quick march. Try this out, but anything around the recommended crotchet = 120 will sound quite active enough and encourage the musical direction towards the first beat of the next bar.

E♭ major is a slightly uncomfortable key to play in, so accuracy will be a challenge. The hands are often moving in contrary motion, so consistent fingering will be essential. In order to consolidate the triplet/duplet rhythm use words as a teaching aid. 'Beefburger, chips and chocolate pan-cakes' quickly establishes the rhythm of triplet quavers and six straight quavers. The ornaments are straightforward and unhurried; take note of the editorial suggestions here.

It is the phrasing that will keep the march marching. The upbeat to each section will need to be kept light and detached, as will most left-hand crotchets. The editorial suggestions are excellent but don't be afraid to try your own solutions. You might like to make all the first few quavers detached and phrase together just the first two of the next grouping. The triplets work well *legato* and, just occasionally, experiment phrasing the first two quavers of later bars to see if it adds rhythmic buoyancy to the piece.

There are no dynamics marked and therefore a strong temptation arises to play it all fairly solidly. Again, use the opportunity to experiment. You might like to start the second section *piano* followed by a *crescendo* to bar 18. The drum-like bars 23 and 24 might be *piano* followed by the two similar bars *forte*. There is no right answer; the only wrong one is no dynamic variety at all.

This is an excellent piece which will encourage a confident and positive start to an exam programme.

A:5 Attwood *Minuetto and 3 variations*

This is an excellent, vibrant and cheerful introduction to variation form from a pupil of Mozart and it would be interesting to compare it with some of the simpler Mozart or Kabalevsky variations. Each variation needs its own distinct character, so you might like to have a bit of fun linking each variation with a different relative or brother/sister as they dance (or run) around the ballroom. The different characters also demand a wide variety of technical skills and so the choice of the tempo will be very important – a balance between an elegant minuet tempo and one that is not too fast for those final semiquavers.

A common problem in examinations will be a performance with three carefully prepared variations all at different speeds, particularly when triplets enter into the equation. Some initial rhythm practice or games may be needed to avoid slowing in Variation 1 and rushing in Variation 2. It is quite useful to play the theme at a top octave on the piano while each variation is being played so that the pupil can more clearly hear the tempo relationships and the way the variations weave their way around the original melody.

The left-hand figures in the Theme and Variation 1 will need to be carefully judged. In the theme a little more emphasis is needed on the bottom notes, with a very light thumb on the D but at the same time lightening all the notes towards the end of the bar. In Variation 1 the left hand will need to *decrescendo* slightly up the triplets to avoid the accompaniment 'beating time'.

Variations 2 and 3 rely on their rests for part of their character, so make sure the hand is lifted exactly at the right time, remembering that there is rhythm in rests as well as notes.

Throughout the whole piece make the most of the wonderful hairpin *crescendi* and *diminuendi*, which will add so much to the musical interest, and take note of the other effective dynamic markings, which should provide some excellent contrast. Listen carefully to the quality of tone and avoid becoming too heavy for the texture and style. Beautifully even and well-articulated semiquavers will bring this piece to a virtuosic and exciting conclusion.

A:6 Handel *Sonatina in B flat*

'Oh no, it's those ornaments again!' – this time three in the first line. Don't let these put you off considering this sprightly, sparkling and scintillating sonatina. A successful performance will certainly require excellent fingers, control and confidence but it is also a real gem of a piece, being both attractive and impressive.

The recommended tempo (crotchet = *c.*126) would achieve a very buoyant and exciting performance, but don't be too swayed by this; you could successfully take it down to crotchet = *c.*108, as long as the piece stays 'on its toes', with effective phrasing and short *staccato*.

Wise pupils will use the rests to prepare for the next phrase, so encourage this from the outset, particularly in bars 3, 4, 8 etc, where any last-minute jumping may lead to unwanted accents and possible hesitation. The ornaments work well as marked although, as always, avoid dropping the arm weight as you play them; this gives the fingers little freedom to move. Instead, let the fingers do the work alone with a relaxed and balanced arm. The most troubling moment will probably be in bar 10, where the ornaments could be left out or just one put in. Don't jeopardize a good performance by putting them in if this results in anxiety or slowing down. Observe all the rests throughout. The point at which you release a note will be just as important as the moment you play it.

A variety of different phrasing will work in this piece. One solution is for the first two quavers to be slurred and the next two played *staccato* and for all upbeat quavers and the left-hand crotchets to be detached, but by all means experiment. If a pupil has access to a harpsichord, or even a harpsichord sound on an electric piano, do try it out. It can often clarify the phrasing wonderfully.

As always, consider the dynamics. I would suggest a good confident tone to start with, a *diminuendo* through bars 3 and 4, then a *crescendo* as the line descends in bars 5 and 6, leading with the bottom notes and matching the left-hand crotchets. The tiniest *rallentando* works well at the end, perhaps with a final, stylish, arpeggiated chord.

B:1 Granados *The Evening Bell*

Granados was still a student when he wrote this atmospheric miniature. Perhaps he submitted it anxiously to his composition professor, hoping for the seal of approval. It certainly succeeds in creating an evocative mood, and a sensitive response to tone colour needs to be part of the pupil's musical nature. It helps to remember that it is intended to be a sketch, a suggestion of a scene, leaning towards impressionist colours.

The notes still have to be cleanly managed, with a clear *cantabile* for the bell each time it appears. Ideally, the melody notes also need *cantabile* projection over the inner right-hand parts. Although this is not a skill that small hands find easy, it is worth a try when the possibility arises.

The few grace notes are best played before the beat and should be gently fitted in with no fuss. Just one arpeggio chord in the second bar indicates that Grandos wanted this harmony to be warmly shown. Pedalling is a major consideration. If pupils have mastered the knack of *legato* pedalling, the sound world of this piece will be much easier than with dabs of direct pedalling. It is marked *con pedale* and without pedal it would not succeed in atmosphere or colour.

Allegretto is faster than the tempo which might be adopted by pupils when thoughtfully mixing their palette of colours. An easy two-in-a-bar stops the piece from sounding too solemn.

Pupils who are lucky enough to have spent a holiday in Spain can enjoy remembering lazy evenings, especially during the final bars of this piece, when examiners will not be nodding off but rather listening attentively to the grading of tone as the bell finally stops and all is still. Keep the moment by moving hands slowly off the keys – the final touch in a piece which needs a sense of performance.

B:2 C. Gurlitt *Allegretto*

These little flowers dance along in a French valse at the opening, a shade faster than the more ponderous 'Blue Danube' kind of waltz. It helps to hum or sing along with the lilting melody, which needs an elegant forward flow, untroubled by audible bar lines. An over-heavy thumb note could cut across the melody when the top line is tied, so keep the weight on the out-side of the hand. *Legato* pedalling helps this section and adds substance to the sustained bass notes.

The middle section, beginning at bar 17, needs only *poco animato*, as the left-hand quavers are not virtuoso runs, just another flowing melody. These passages can be phrased as musically as the right-hand lines, providing the fingers are firm. Stable fingering and lots of separate work will make this reliable but, with all the activity going on in the bass line, make sure the right-hand rests are exact lengths and that the chords are not out-staying their welcome, a frequent problem in this kind of passage.

The return of the *con anima* melody announces the final section. Since all music needs to be played *con anima* (with feeling), it is surprising how rarely these words are actually written in the score. Those who might play this *senza anima* should be guided to another choice.

B:3 S. Heller *Study in D*

This is *giocoso* not *furioso*! We are all familiar with Heller in his lyrical style but, apart from bars 23–32, there is no sign of his usual *legato* lines. Due to the B minor opening and *staccato* dots in all directions, it would be possible to get a mistaken idea of the mood but this is a fun piece with lots of energy and immediate appeal.

There is quite a challenge in the *staccato* precision, which has to be maintained crisply throughout. Adolescents with long flexible fingers might find that the essential neatness is hard to achieve. If there is a light of excitement in the pupil's eyes when the piece is played to them, it's an invaluable sign that the fire to master the music will carry them through the practice process.

Despite the vigorous onrush – and this will sound tame if taken at too conservative a tempo – there is plenty of variety and all the markings are important if the possibilities are to be fully explored. At the necessary lively pace, it is helpful to keep as close as possible to the keys, thinking slightly ahead for the changes of position and dynamics.

The finger changes on the first F♯s and similar suggestions seem fussy at speed but may help to keep the repeated notes really crisp.

Studies are all meant to improve some aspect of technique and, apart from a huge amount of *staccato*, there are also contrasts of articulation between the hands, occasional *legato* upper lines at the same time as detached work and plenty of detail, all of which adds life to the piece and is much appreciated by examiners.

The *risoluto* at bar 53 braces us for the final stages and the climax at bar 60 needs obvious pointing so that the *legato* left-hand melody at bars 64–72 will come as a complete surprise.

There will be great satisfaction when the last two chords are dropped precisely and lightly into place at the end of this enjoyable dose of musical medicine.

B:4 Glière *Song*

This is a warm, Romantic song that will suit the more musically mature and technically accomplished of your pupils. Any singers amongst them should find it very easy to put some words to this melody, instinctively understanding the phrase shapes and allowing flexibility and time at the ends of phrases for a breath.

Equally, if you have a budding organist then they will find the sustained and *legato* accompanying harmonies familiar territory. The use of substitution, changing from one finger to another on a held note, is a very common organ technique and will be invaluable in achieving a warm bed of Romantic harmonies to support the melody, allowing the pedal absolute freedom to change. If you have a pupil who is both a singer *and* an organist then you're on to a winner.

Technically, the piece will need a pupil who is comfortable projecting a melodic line with the top fingers of one hand whilst holding gently moving accompanying notes underneath. There are a lot of held notes which form an essential part of the harmony and which may be missed if the pupil is not observant. Fingering needs to be carefully considered otherwise the intricacies may well get the fingers into a tangle. It will also be essential in achieving a smooth *legato* through all the chromatic left-hand quavers. Rest assured, however: this is a slow, reflective song and a natural musical flexibility will help ease the way around some of the tricky corners.

The pedal will need to be entirely independent of the necessity to hold the notes. It should simply provide a warmth and colour to the piece, changing each minim beat in the first line for instance. The fingers should ensure that the bottom F or lower notes in the right hand are not lost when the changes occur.

Explore the full dynamic range, keeping the wrists relaxed and forgiving so that the sound doesn't become too percussive, and generally keep the texture light. The *ritenuto* at the end gives plenty of time sensitively to shape the conclusion of the song.

B:5 Grieg *Dance of the Elves*

This is a wonderfully imaginative piece by Norway's musical equivalent of Tolkien. Indeed, those pupils who have read *The Hobbit* or *The Lord of the Rings* will have an instant picture of the unfolding events in this piece. It is a wonderful illustration of Grieg's ability to tell fantasy stories in music.

The piece needs some very particular sounds and colours to really bring it to life. In general, keep all the chords light – these are elves, not gnomes or dwarves. (They have their own pieces.) The best way to approach the music is to hear the sound you want in your head first, then experiment to see how it can be achieved. The chords in the opening need very active finger tips close to the keys and a relaxed arm to get a precise, light *staccato*. The pupil will also need to balance the chords carefully so that they don't become too thick. Notice that the melody, such as it is, is not always in the upper part (bars 7, 8 etc) and check the final bars before deciding the *pianissimo* dynamic, as it must leave sufficient scope for a reliable *molto pianissimo* at the end.

The elves themselves are in a mischievous mood here and so is the composer, who does his utmost to catch the pianist and listener out. Have a look at bars 17–22 for instance; these require an elvish ability to leap in both hands. Look also at the wide variety of dynamic contrast and phrasing that Grieg asks for within such a short space of time. Without these the piece would lose much of its character and wicked sense of humour, but thankfully the various repeats mean that any hard work done in the opening bars is rewarded in triplicate later on.

Don't worry too much if you can't quite match an athletic dotted minim = *c*.76 (given as a suggestion at the end of the music); if you are getting the right sort of sound and phrasing, dotted minim = 72 or 69 will work just as well and still lead to a convincing and fantasy-land performance.

B:6 Schumann *Reaper's Song*

Schumann wrote over 300 songs so it is no surprise that he composed a few without words for piano, of which this is one, although it is also rather more than this, portraying an idyllic country scene. This is harvesting in the 'olden' days – no combine harvesters and tractors here. Instead, imagine fields of golden corn and men and women with their scythes, singing a very beautiful and uplifting song to keep their rhythm going and their spirits up. The middle unison section is definitely much more masculine, the opening and bars 21 to 28 much more feminine. The final few bars perhaps convey the sound of distant hunting horns.

The warmth of the sun needs to pervade the music through use of pedal and rich harmonies. It is essential to hold all the tied notes for their full length with the fingers and there is scope to use the pedal a little more frequently than suggested. Keep the piece gentle. The tempo marked on this edition, whilst substantially slower than that on Clara Schumann's (see footnote to music), could still be a notch more expansive if you feel this suits the music.

Don't over-accent the accents; keep them subtle, 'leaning' into them, and all within the context of the dynamic. The grace notes should be kept light and unpanicked. The middle section, while loud, needs a lot of dynamic shape to give it musical direction, or the quavers will sound too mechanical and deliberate. A very good *legato* will really help and contrast well with the final few bars which should have a light and crisp *staccato*. Bars 5 to 8 are almost a duet. Experiment bringing out the middle line a little more, then the top line, and decide on the balance you prefer.

As in every song, don't forget to allow the singers to breathe between phrases. Schumann has indicated these moments by using quaver rests, so do observe them. This is a musically rewarding and very beautiful piece that demands little technical athleticism and will inspire pupils with a good imagination.

C:1 Bartók *Jeering Song*

A spirited burst of playground beastliness, which will be easy for pupils to understand. Hungarian children may be more at home with changing bar lengths but this is more a matter of the right feeling for the rhythm, once the counting has been worked out. Conjuring up an image of an unpopular bully will immediately set the scene. Adults will notice the *ironico* indication with amusement but the implication will be lost on most youngsters.

A huge range of dynamics is required to bring this off with full impact and, for once, a hint of harshness in the loudest levels will not come amiss. The tempo needs to be brisk and, despite the obvious title, there's more than a hint of a national dance, given added kick with the accents, sometimes on the off-beat.

Hands must be exactly together, not too difficult at the start but keep the precision when the left-hand melody begins at bar 13. This passage should be much lighter, (perhaps the girls are joining in), so fingers need a firm, crisp attack to avoid misfires when notes fail to speak. The low bass quavers could be particularly prone to this sort of mishap. Keeping close to the keys for the *staccato* makes for control, especially at speed.

The *ossia* alternative ornaments, like musical sneers, are only for the very accomplished. The effect will still work without the grace notes and a loss of tempo would spoil the momentum. Sensible fingering suggestions are printed for the left-hand chords, which keep the basic hand position and help to avoid smudges. Watch for clef changes and listen for the balance of hands, so that the accompanying chords allow the melody to sing out, especially in the quieter passages. The last two bars look strange on the page but the quavers start on the first beat.

A brilliant choice for directing nervous energy into the music and gleeful fun to imagine one of the less sentimental scenes from childhood.

C:2 Terence Greaves *Baa, Baa, Blue Sheep's Waltz*

This witty title refers to a melancholy state of mind, not a recent baptism in a sheep dip! The *lento doloroso* tempo and falling semitones in the right-hand chords give the basic feel but, like all slow pieces, things musn't get too indulgent. The piece is carefully marked with *poco ritardando*, *a tempo*, various commas, precise dynamics and even some *una corda* pedal, used from bar 33 to the end. With all these musical instructions we don't have to guess what the composer meant, although he would no doubt tell us himself if we asked, as he is one of our team of examiners.

Several skills are needed, apart from a relaxed feel for the style and command of a suitable range of nightclub tone colour. The right hand sometimes has to sing out the plaintive dotted minims with a good *cantabile* tone, whilst also gently filling in the chords. Left-hand arpeggio accompaniment patterns should have their warmest tone on the first beat of the bar and give a rich background at the various dynamic levels. Pupils with tense shoulders and arms would find these technical subtleties hard to manage, so this piece is a marvellous chance to encourage anxious youngsters to relax and enjoy the squelchy sounds, which will also be useful in other more serious contexts. With quite different harmonies, Brahms often needs a similar sonority. The piece is marked *con pedale* and it would be impossible to manage a really convincing sound without the pedal, preferably used in the *legato* patterns.

Give the left-hand quavers an expressive rise and fall in the section which starts at bar 21 and follow this with gentle chords from bar 29, squeezing the right-hand outside fingers so that the melody sings out a little more than the rest of the texture. The octaves from bar 33 should be very light and the *una corda* pedal helps to blur the edges still further.

The final instructions are a graduated *ritardando, più lento* and *molto ritardando*, ensuring that the piece does not run out of momentum too soon. Those of us who know Terence are aware of his wonderful sense of humour and, although this is an extremely effective tearjerker of a piece, it wouldn't surprise me if the final bar is the last 'baa'.

C:3 Kabalevsky *Sad Story*

Weary resignation is not usually associated with childhood but this one seems to have both these qualities. An imaginative pupil could create a mental picture and a story to lift the notes off the page.

The hypnotic, repetitive rhythm suggests a working song (perhaps of a small, cold Russian child in a bare landscape) but there are some brighter moments and it does end with a major chord. Notice also that the suggested metronome mark sets a flowing momentum which helps the right-hand *cantabile* to keep its vitality.

Clefs are not always as expected, a frequent trap for pupils in the early stages of learning a new piece. Coloured highlighter pens are useful hazard warnings, particularly if applied by the pupils themselves. Experienced pianists frequently cover their scores in stabs, slashes and digs – anything that will help the performance is fine; exam books are, after all, working copies.

Expressive phrasing – as obvious as you like – and a wide tonal range make this a more substantial piece than its single page would indicate. A strong, regular basic beat underpins the melody but there is a potential trap in the dotted crotchet–quaver rhythm in bars 6, 8 and 22. Some pupils will play the quavers either too soon or too late.

A new idea appears at bar 17, then the most dramatic passage immediately follows, from bar 25. The left hand has to cover quite large distances here, so it will be important to have an accurate aim for the lower fifth on F and C, plus a memory of the upper chords if the tempo is to be kept intact. *Legato* pedalling helps a lot at this point and it's worth noticing that the pedal captures the low F in bar 32 and goes on a little longer than the final chord. Try to get the hands exactly together here and think of the whole shape of the chord rather than a collection of individual notes, creating a controlled end to a powerful little scene.

C:4 Alan Haughton *You and Me*

This will prove an understandably popular choice with many pupils and rightly so. Alan Haughton composed a lot of very contrasting and effective pieces for young pupils and this one is a favourite.

The title not only fits well to the chords at the beginning of bar 2 (and will help encourage lazy hands to keep the final quaver short) but possibly also refers to the two halves of the piece. The first half (bars 1 to 10) is the 'head' – a fairly straight run of the tune. The second half is improvisatory and has a very authentic jazz feel to it.

From bar 3 the piece has a strong rhythmic drive, provided by the repeating left hand, which is predictable and very comfortable to play, leaving the performer plenty of time to concentrate on the right-hand melody. The main problems will be mastering the 'swing' rhythm and, particularly, the rhythm of the opening.

You can think of the piece in 12/8 throughout to give you some idea of the rhythms but, sadly, this is only half the solution. Swung jazz is 'caught' (like a cold), so some listening is essential if your pupils have no experience of this style. Others who play regularly in a big band or school jazz band will probably instinctively swing everything and need little encouragement. The opening bars will cause the most frustration; they are particularly confusing as the rhythm is different at the beginning of bar 2. Ignore the ties for a while until the rhythm is secure, then simply avoid lifting the hands.

The character of the piece will be greatly enhanced if the phrasing is carefully observed. If the phrase finishes on a quaver then keep it very short but light (unless marked with an accent). Show all the rests throughout, lifting any chords absolutely together, and keep the grace note light. It works well rather squashed into the chord, almost as part of the chord but released immediately.

Note the *sempre staccato* marking in the left hand; this will also mean that all the chords in bar 9 are short.

It is possible that many performances will be marred by an enthusiastic but rather forceful approach to the piece. Observe the dynamic markings but notice that the opening is only *forte* and that the piece actually sounds at its best if it is not all too loud. Instead, 'warm-up' the chords with a dab of pedal, if the pupil feels comfortable with this, and bring out the humour in the performance.

No cheating on those final notes by taking too much time. It's quite a jump so hands will need to travel quickly; why not encourage pupils to learn the last bar from memory so that they can look at their hands? In fact, why not learn the whole piece from memory as an experiment? (No need to play from memory in the exam.) It will give a great sense of freedom and enhance the improvisatory nature of the piece.

C:5 William Mathias *Burlesque*

A piece for the showoffs amongst your pupils and not that hard if it is prepared slowly and patiently. Those of you who know the music of Villa-Lobos will not find it so unusual to be playing in the one hand on white notes, in the other on black. You will also know that this often means the piece looks a lot trickier than it is and this is certainly the case here. The hands have only a couple of small jumps but are generally covering the same group of notes for some time. The only technical demand is the stamina to be able to play so much *staccato* for so long in the treble register of the piano.

A burlesque is a humorous piece often involving grotesque exaggeration. This burlesque fits the bill exactly. Exaggerate all the phrasing, keeping the *staccato* very short and energetic (the whole piece is marked *forte*) and placing the *tenuto* notes slightly (bars 2, 4 etc), as if stamping your foot in a lively dance – not too heavily though, because the left hand makes even more of an issue out of it in bars 12 and 13.

The little phrase markings over the quavers are essential to give the piece extra character and the opening mordents will work far better on the beat than before. The grace notes in bars 5 and 7 swoop up to the top note having established the lower. Think of it as a violinist's *portamento*.

The tempo marking is *fast* – perhaps a touch ambitious for some pupils. The piece will still work at a slower tempo if the phrasing is very buoyant. At the faster tempo the piece really comes alive; just remember that there is an *accelerando* marked at the end and a *crescendo*, so don't be too loud or too fast. One little cheat worth trying; drop the dynamic down to *mezzo forte* just where the hairpin starts and then immediately begin to *crescendo*. The excitement generated will easily excuse this change and with no *ritardando* and very short crotchets it is an ending which will 'bring the house down' at any concert.

C:6 Pamela Wedgwood *Laid-back Blues*

Every teacher will remember the times they have spent persuading a pupil *not* to play the rhythm dotted quaver–semiquaver as crotchet–quaver triplet. Well here is the perfect piece for that pupil, in which they can forget everything you have told them and swing a lazy triplet on those dotted rhythms for an authentic jazz feel. It's a 'cool' piece and will prove very popular but avoid giving it to the impatient, as any hint of rushing will spoil the mood. It really needs to sound . . . well . . . laid-back!

The tempo marking is perfect and all the quavers and dotted rhythms should be 'swung' throughout (thought of as triplets). This may seem confusing in bars 9, 10 etc, but don't let this worry you; it is a notational difference but very little different in practice. Rests need to be carefully observed and counted, particularly in bar 25 where there will be a strong urge to come in early. In fact, very slightly elongating the rests here may highlight the rather cheeky character but must be carefully judged. Check the rhythm in bar 24, which may need a little help.

Hold all longer and tied notes for their full value. The chords in bars 9, 10 etc should all be held under the right-hand melody, as should the strong left-hand notes in bars 17 to 25, where a more 'heavy rock' band tries to get the party moving.

It is important to remember that, at this tempo, too short a *staccato* will be out of character; instead, a more smoochy and gentle *staccato* is more in keeping with the blues tradition, as is some use of the pedal. There is no pedal marked so you don't have to use any but it really does improve the performance in some bars, so if possible give it a go. You might like to try some in the opening (and similar) bars, perhaps down on the first beat then up with the hands in beat three. Bars 9–11, 13 and 14 could be subtly pedalled on the second and fourth beats, making sure the right hand has phrased off before putting the pedal down. This will help achieve a warm *legato* in the left hand without obscuring the phrasing.

Well-observed dynamics will enhance the piece further, particularly in the last line where they will provide the ultimate cheeky ending.

GRADE 5

Grade 5 is a watershed between the early grades and those beyond the necessary hurdle of Grade 5 Theory or Practical Musicianship. Hopefully, the extra demands, both technical and musical, have been gradually approached through the preceding years and it will be apparent to teachers which of their pupils is capable of progressing successfully on to the later grades and which might be reaching their natural limits. In either case, enjoyable performances of the pieces for this grade indicate a real ability to play, rather than just early attempts at the instrument.

LIST A
The pieces by both Bachs repay careful effort. The Handel minuet is slightly easier but does need some ornamentation for full effect. The anonymous 'Allegro Moderato' is a lively show piece and the Purcell, although not flamboyant, still needs good independence of hands. The Kuhlau will suit pupils with an eye for detail and sense of humour. Don't be put off by its length.

LIST B
The Glière 'Rondo' and 'Little Piece in C sharp minor' by Franck are both a little more demanding of technical rather than interpretative skills but in very different ways. The opposite is the case with 'The Orphan Girl' and the Skryabin 'Prelude in D flat'; both need good pedalling skills and musical insight. The Dvořák is a real character piece, full of contrast, and 'By the Brook' is relatively straightforward, once the technique is mastered.

LIST C
'Castles in the Air' has few real difficulties in the technique but needs tonal imagination, while those who choose the Bartók need quick reactions and a cool nerve. The Berkeley piece is more comfortable to play than it looks, and Richard Rodney Bennett's 'Diversion No. 2' is also charming and approachable. 'SAZZ' and 'I Got Plenty o' Nuttin'' need to be well matched to the pupil's natural style.

A:1 Anon. *Allegro Moderato*

This is a wonderful, lively and buoyant piece that must have amused and entertained the young Mozart. It is the perfect piece with which to show off to relatives, with its hand crossing and vibrant, energetic semiquavers. There is, in fact, a very similar variation in Wolfgang Mozart's own variations on 'Ah, vous dirai-je Maman' (KV300e).

The hand crossing will involve a lot of forward thinking and accuracy and will almost certainly be easier if learnt from memory. Practise the opening with the left hand static over its first few notes (and not actually playing anything) while the right hand jumps across; this will get the hands used to the sensation of crossing. Then play the left hand as a chord with the right hand and, if this is too easy, try with the eyes shut. Finally, separate the left hand as marked. The right hand will need to move the moment it has played its note, so in general keep the crotchets short.

In bars where the hands are not crossing, slightly emphasize the bottom notes of the semiquaver figures (bars 9, 10 etc) and phrase them with the left hand keeping the upbeats of the bar light.

The semiquavers will need a lot of careful and separate practice to get them absolutely even. Accenting every other note and then swapping around will help the control and practising in rhythms may be necessary to quicken them up. The biggest danger will be that the top repeated notes are too heavy, so keep the hand fairly still and slightly weighted towards the weaker fingers. Once the technique is mastered, however, then the piece virtually plays itself. Try the editorial dynamics or explore some of your own but don't forget that a piece like this has charm and humour so avoid 'driving' the music forward and keep it light.

The tempo marking is sensible but if you can manage it a touch faster then it will add to the sparkle and the performance will deserve a standing ovation.

A:2 Kuhlau *Allegro*

This is a delightful 'Puckish' movement, full of comic ballet and humour. At first sight you may be alarmed by the apparent length of this piece but don't be. The first section to bar 36 is in three sections, the end a repeat of the beginning; this whole section is then repeated at the end. The middle section is also made up of three sections of almost identical material. If the architecture of the piece is well understood then it will be easier to learn and begin to make musical sense. The length of the piece will mean that good concentration will be essential, so consider this when making your choice.

Kuhlau was a Danish composer well known for his flute music and the articulation and texture of this allegro suggests that the composer may well have had the flute in mind. Take note of the many phrase markings, keeping the *staccato* light and giving every part of the musical line shape and musical direction. The *staccato* is best achieved from the surface of the keys with active finger tips – anything more weighty than a finger *staccato* will lose the performance its buoyancy. Attention to detail will greatly enhance the performance and careful listening is essential. Be careful not to accent the first note of each short phrase in bars 20 to 22 and similar bars; show all left-hand rests and keep the semiquavers absolutely even.

Avoid over-accenting the marked accents; treat them expressively in context. All passage work should be carefully and sensitively shaped to prevent it sounding too mechanical and left-hand accompaniment figures, such as those in bars 37–43, must be unobtrusive. I would use the editorial dynamic markings as a guide here, noticing the *crescendi* and *diminuendi* and using them to give the piece musical direction and interest; the *smorzando* in bar 46 could be especially effective. Give musical direction to all the repeated chords and notes, which will generally lead towards the first beat of the next bar.

Finally, listen very carefully to the balance throughout. The right hand will need to be well projected and the left hand kept light, particularly in bars 37–44 and similar passages.

A:3 Purcell *Prelude in C*

The term 'prelude' was often loosely attached to an improvisation which preceded a play, ceremony or, in this case, a suite of dances. Imagine Purcell enjoying trying out the touch (and tuning) of a two-manual harpsichord – putting it through its paces – some two-part counterpoint here, a few runs there, fanfare-like chords and then a few chordal and imitative sequences. And all based on the same opening theme. Here you have a flamboyant, exuberant beginning to a concert and hardly a black note in sight (or white note in the case of a harpsichord!).

This doesn't mean that the piece is technically straightforward. In fact, there are some tricky moments and fingers will need to be thoroughly coached to ensure they don't go astray. Make absolutely sure all fingering is consistent and highlight particular bars for practice.

The piece begins ominously like a two-part invention, so some separate practice will be needed to gain sufficient independence of the hands but don't let this worry you. Notice bars 4, 9–11, 16–18 and 22, where the hands are much less independent – a good point at which to steady the nerve and relax until the next moment of Purcell's inspiration. The passage to look at first is undoubtedly the final 12 bars, where the 'knitting' needs to be studied, the fingering carefully considered (particularly the substitution) and all notes held for their full value but no longer.

The piece needs plenty of buoyancy and life, so detach most of the quavers and avoid too many accents in order to maintain the musical direction. It will also be essential to give all of the semiquaver passages plenty of dynamic shaping and contrast, remembering not to get too heavy and strident. It mustn't sound like a study.

The tempo marking is very sensible but a more courageous and technically fluent pianist may well like to try it a little faster. Think of it as a piece for two trumpets and organ, ensuring it is full of fun, grandeur and technical ease.

A:4 J. C. F. Bach *Allegretto in F*

'Lovely piece but what about the ornaments?' Many teachers will have these thoughts, as the appearance of these worrying little signs can spoil an otherwise tempting melody. Any doubts about the Board's policy regarding ornaments should be dispelled by reference to the disclaimer on the first page of all the albums of graded pieces.

Examiners are all too familiar with the kind of performance that slows down at every trill or turn, rather like the effect of 'sleeping policemen' on a suburban road. Don't let these anxieties put you off this delightful allegretto, as it has a lovely melody, comfortable left-hand accompaniment, straightforward phrasing and some addictive moments in the harmonic progressions.

Try playing the piece without ornaments until the allegretto tempo is established and the notes are reasonably safe. If ornaments are added before the fundamental rhythm is in the pupil's system, problems with laborious playing of these corners set in with a vengeance.

Performances without ornaments are acceptable in the lower grades, providing the playing is well-managed overall, especially when the tempo is on the fast side. In this piece, however, some of the turns and appoggiaturas are quite easy and can be managed without danger to the rhythm.

The first turn at bar 5 works well but the following turn in the same bar could be omitted, without any loss of style. The same applies in bar 6 and similar passages later. Four turns in two bars is a bit optimistic for most

Grade 5 candidates. At bar 8 it is fine to play just the appoggiatura and not the mordent and these four semiquavers can relax just a touch into the return of the theme. The trill in bar 17 could be reduced to a mordent on the beat, or left out. There is no difficulty in playing the quaver appoggiatura in bar 26, if you like the effect.

Apart from these details, the only other awkward moment could be at bars 16 and 36, when the right hand has to jump to the E and B♭ chord, without a hiccup in the shape. If this causes repeated accidents and doesn't respond to treatment, it would be better to leave out the B♭, especially as it appears in the next chord, which is much easier to control.

The melody sings out in elegant phrases above a gentle accompaniment, which could be enhanced with little touches of pedal but only when the left hand is in semiquaver chord shapes. Any more pedal would blur the texture, and clarity of articulation is part of the charm of the piece.

The musical-box opening melody and light-footed phrases are punctuated by commas but these do not mean breaks in the continuity of the music. Much of this piece depends upon musical phrasing and a sense of poise which these commas help, as they indicate places where the music needs to take a small breath between phrases. This is the kind of piece that is frequently played in television costume dramas, when one of the characters goes to the piano and entertains the party after dinner. In a modern context it could be just as charming.

A:5 J. S. Bach *Prelude No. 4 in D*

Some early planning of the route before setting out is recommended for this piece. A glance at the footnote opens up a Pandora's Box of phrasing decisions about the opening subject. Realistic teachers will know that the notes of this piece are challenging enough, without fussing about details of articulation, but if these refinements are to be considered eventually, it's better to do so right from the start.

Fingers need to memorize the differences of attack caused by detaching some notes and to be able to repeat the same phrasing when similar material returns. The left-hand quavers may be detached or *legato*; there will be no advantage in marks either way. The most important considerations will be secure independence of hands and good co-ordination of the two or three parts.

This is a piece for the technically confident pupil, who is unlikely to lose his or her composure in the exam. When a slip happens, it is difficult to pick up the pieces if the continuity of physical memory is upset. On the brighter side, once this jaunty prelude is really in the system, it is satisfying to play and is of the musical quality to be expected from its composer. It is quite possible to have two-in-a-bar vitality without pushing the tempo into the danger zone and a speed limit of around crotchet = 84 would be wise.

Holding the tied notes means less freedom of action for the other fingers, so small hands would be especially taxed at bar 27 (where the printed fingering adds to the problems; use 4th on the first right-hand A of this bar). The change from 3 to 5 on the held E minim of bar 31 is awkward at speed and I suspect that only a few candidates will surprise examiners by holding all sustained lines for their exact length.

No dynamics are marked and, with so much activity in the lines, many listeners will not miss strong tonal contrasts. Phrasing does, as ever, need a sense of direction and the natural fluctuations of pitch avoid a deadpan impression. Think of the two main sections as each having its own start, main point and end. The left hand contributes as much to this kind of shaping as the right hand.

Examiners will be delighted by a buoyant, sustained tempo, neat articulation and a natural sense of phrasing but these performances will be a rare pleasure. Last time this piece was set, we heard many rather cautious accounts, with many a slip but, nevertheless, time spent in the company of J. S. Bach, mastering his notes, even at a slowish tempo, will have helped the candidate's overall progress considerably.

A:6 Handel *Minuet in G minor*

Gilding the lily is more of an issue in this dignified minuet than in faster-moving Baroque pieces. The clean lines and large intervals are strong enough to stand alone but there is no doubt that some ornaments add style and grace.

The suggested appoggiaturas are easily included and should be emphasized for their full effect. After that, it's a case of selecting mordents and trills to your taste, with the technical capabilities of each pupil in mind. The measured trills at bars 19, 27 and 36 could be the starting point in the process of choice and may well be the only trills played. Mordents, on the beat, are extra frills to be enjoyed rather than imposed.

The dance needs to set out as it means to go on, with a stately measured tread and extra energy on each first beat of the bar. If there are three equally weighted crotchets, the effect will be more like a dancer in wellington boots.

Some dynamic planning is helpful to emphasize the shapes of sections and this is also left to your taste. A positive opening, with the four-bar phrases kept in mind, could be followed by a quieter start at bar 9, where Handel has already decorated the second beat. Rises in pitch naturally grow in tone and this will happen at the end of the first main part. Similar marking of the starts and ends of phrases will enhance the second half.

Pupils often like to choose their own dynamics, once given some guide-lines, and it always makes the music feel more their own. Teachers playing various different tonal levels and asking 'Do you prefer this – or this?' will awaken the kind of listening that musicians use all the time, quite apart from its value in the aural tests.

The undecorated notes are not demanding but keep an ear on the held left-hand notes; they support the otherwise spare texture. There are also some dotted minims in the right hand from bar 31 that might be overlooked.

Formal dancing is a world away from most pupils' experience but a picture of a wonderful ballroom and gorgeously costumed dancers can give that vital spark of inspiration, which will transform a performance and move the player closer to the mysterious term 'style'.

B:1 Granados *The Orphan Girl*

This is a rather poignant title. Granados and his wife died on the way back from the première of his opera *Goya* when the ship they were on was tor-pedoed in the English Channel. He didn't leave an orphaned daughter but did leave an orphaned son (Edward). It is a very beautiful, haunting piece, with a plaintive melody, yet full of Spanish atmosphere and character.

Think of the piece as a song with guitar accompaniment. To obtain a resonating, guitar-like colour in the left hand the piece will need to be sensitively pedalled, changing with every change of harmony. The little guitar-like decorations in bars 4, 8, 10 etc, need careful consideration. You might like to give a slightly undamped effect using half-pedal, or alterna-tively giving small dabs of pedal. The old adage 'pedalling with the ears' definitely applies here. It will also be essential to hold all notes with the fingers, otherwise changes of pedal will lose the harmonic support. Practise without the pedal for a while to educate this into the fingers.

There are effectively only eight bars of music but the performance needs to be sensitively judged with plenty of space, shape and colour. Any intrusive accents will spoil the line and a pupil will need to be particularly aware of this in bars 3, 7 etc, where jumping the hand on the sixths amidst semiquavers may well cause an unwanted bump. Be careful also in the left hand, bars 10, 14 etc, and on the little left-hand mordents which by their very nature will provide their own emphasis.

The dynamic marking is *piano* throughout but remember that this is a range of dynamic and there is a *diminuendo* at the end. I suspect Granados is simply pleading with the performer not to get too loud. I would be careful not to begin too tentatively; many fine performances have been spoilt when a performer has lost confidence once the first notes of a piece have failed to speak. On what may be an unfamiliar piano, begin with plenty of weight but with a slow attack; this will ensure a positive beginning.

An instinctively musical performer will want to take a little time placing the change of harmony in bar 12 but save this for the end; the *rallentando* and *diminuendo* could make the final major chord very special. Give plenty of time on the pause.

B:2 Skryabin *Prelude in D flat*

Skryabin wrote around 80 preludes and was deeply influenced by Chopin. It would be interesting to compare this prelude with some of Chopin's own and perhaps also with the Purcell prelude in list A. By the Romantic period, a prelude had become much more a work in its own right.

This is an intensely personal composition, suiting a musical and sensitive performer and demanding maturity and command of pianistic colour. The pupil will need to concentrate on images and feelings rather than tunes. The almost key-less opening might be a distant memory or musical question mark, later conjuring up the image of a misty, lonely landscape or memories of a passing conversation. The slightly intangible melody could be a soaring bird or evoke a fleeting emotion, and the final chord the warmth of knowing we are secure and falling into a deep sleep.

The left hand will need a lot of practice without pedal, making sure it is beautifully *legato* and seamless. If you can't join both notes then make sure one at least is joined. No intrusive accents should spoil the still atmosphere; the first chord of each short phrase will need to be 'floated' in with a light arm. Hold all the semibreves for their full length. Any shortening of their value will make the piece sound rather hurried. There is scope, however, for the left-hand quavers to gather a little musical direction through bars 5 to 8 as long as it is subtly done.

The right hand should be well projected and beautifully shaped. Allow the left hand to take over in bar 17 but don't force the accents here; it's expressive and really highlights the shape of the phrase. The tempo marking gives the piece plenty of musical direction but if your pupil is listening well and has good control then a slightly slower tempo is possible.

Pupils should consider using the pedal; it will need to be changed frequently and gently in the opening bars. There is only really time for the tiniest of dabs of half-pedal on the quavers but do pedal the long notes to achieve a warm colour. Once the right hand has entered, the pedal can be changed every two beats.

This wonderful prelude is a masterpiece and worth every minute of effort. The piece has never quite established the key throughout and that final D♭ major chord is one of the most spell-binding moments you will hear in a performance; you should be able to hear a pin drop for several seconds after the hands have been gently lifted.

B:3 Karganov *By the Brook*

This is an apt title. The brook chatters away merrily: no cares, no worries, just a naïve innocence. The piece itself, though, is not quite so innocent. Anything less than absolutely even and technically fluent semiquavers will result in a few too many waterfalls, rapids and eddies. On the other hand, it mustn't sound like a study: all the dynamics need to be carefully graded and the pulse allowed some flexibility.

The first thing to master is the technique. Light arms (particularly a light thumb), relaxed wrists and forearms will be important and if your pupil is prone to tension problems in this area then it is probably better to steer them towards one of the other choices. Once the technique is comfortable, however, the piece will almost play itself (almost!) as plenty of the phrases are repeated and the middle section is in fact a written-out repeat of three lines.

Practise as two-note chords throughout (except bar 48 of course); this will serve two purposes, the first to teach the hands where they are going, the second to help the pupil understand the shape of the music. Practising the piece in different rhythms will help speed up the fingers. You could try turning the first note of each pair into a dotted quaver, with three crotchet beats in a bar. Use the longer note as a chance to relax and prepare the right hand for the next bar. Another practice technique is to accent alternate semiquavers with the finger (not by using the arm), thus helping the tonal control. Do this first with the first note of each pair, then with the second. One of the main dangers will be a heavy right-hand thumb, so be aware of this when practising.

Explore the dynamic markings but be conscious of the thin, bright texture. Find your pupil's best *forte* tone and grade all other dynamics accordingly. The phrase markings are not to be taken too literally but, if the hands do not release their second note quickly enough, the piece will lose its sparkle and you will find fingers occupying notes that need to be played again.

The final performance will need a good awareness of the hidden line – essentially the top notes of each group across the bar line – to give it shape. A little bit more 'ping' in the 4th and 5th fingers will help brighten these notes. Some use of pedal will also contribute to the final effect, although the piece could be performed without. Finish with a very cheeky and light *staccato* on the chords.

B:4 Dvořák *Grandpa Dances with Grandma*

When the examiner asks 'Which pieces are you going to play?' many candidates bravely struggle to pronounce the title printed on the music, sometimes with peculiar but endearing results. Not many will attempt this one in the original but the comforting translation tells us exactly what is happening.

The ternary form begins and ends with a nostalgic G minor figure, suggesting the slightly arthritic dance. Memories of more vigorous days are stirred by the middle section – perhaps Grandpa was in military uniform – before we return to the present with a *da capo.*

There is sometimes confusion about repeats and *da capos* in exams. Repeats are not required but *da capos* usually are, unless the examiner asks for them to be omitted. Sometimes this is necessary because of time pressures.

The tender, repeated opening scene seems to depict the twirl of a dance and the suggested fingering is the most comfortable solution, helping to prevent uneven starts to the groups. Matching the tone after tied notes will be important in bars 1 and 2 and the left hand can help to show the pulse by gently emphasizing the first semiquavers. As this is a dance, there is a strict tempo throughout; too much *rubato* would upset the dancers.

Various dynamic markings indicate exactly what to do but tonal levels always convey more than just quiet and loud playing. Think in terms of more energy and confidence for the *forte* phrase starting at bar 9 and a gentler, more thoughtful approach for the *piano* at bar 17. Smoothly graded tone, with lighter second and third beats, will shape the sections and the little mordents should be very light, to avoid a bump on the last quavers.

The sparkle of the middle section, starting at bar 25, needs crisp rhythm and exactly the same tempo. Make the most of the detached dotted chords, followed by the smooth *legato* bars, where the top line could be joined by the outer fingers. A more sensible fingering than that printed at this point could be 5/1, 4/1, 3/1, 4/1, 2/1.

Touches of direct pedalling, just on the first two quavers in each bar of the main sections, prevent blurring but pupils who are at home with *legato* pedalling could change on the first and third beats. To provide contrast, the middle section could be unpedalled, except for dabs of pedal on the first beats; if you choose *legato* pedalling, however, change every quaver in bars 27–28, 31–32 and 39–40 to prevent smudges.

With obliging grandparents, this piece could be brought to life in the pupil's sitting room, giving all concerned a lot of fun and bringing home the need to keep a strong beat when playing music for dancers, whatever their age!

B:5 Franck *Little Piece in C sharp minor*

Intended originally for the harmonium, this piece was designed for players adept at finger *legato* while pedalling vigorously to keep the flow of air going through the instrument – a triumph of co-ordination, fortunately *not* required by candidates who choose this delicate breath of French air.

Pedal, in the piano sense, is best omitted. There are too many chromatic traps for all but the most skilful and the main issue here is the use of finger *legato* in each hand.

In several bars the first beat lies in the left hand, while the right hand is silent, so these moments need a gentle nudge – not a bump – to keep the rhythmic shape intact. This is a feature of the opening phrase, where the left-hand crotchets form an eloquent foundation to the treble quavers, which weave around the harmonic structure.

It is not immediately clear when looking at the page where the main phrase points occur but try building towards the first beat of bar 3 and then falling gently away. The next peak is at bar 8, then a longer phrase leads to bar 16.

Sempre pianissimo at bar 17 introduces an even more subtle colour which then gradually builds to the climax of the whole piece at bar 29. It is worth keeping this *mezzo forte* in mind while building up to this point, as the range of dynamics is quite restrained and it would overpower the piece to be too positive too soon.

All this takes quite a lot of control, as does the part-playing in each hand. A clean *legato*, with no unintentional overlapping, whilst holding a sustained note in the same hand, is quite demanding but is part of the essence of the style. Lots of slow, careful practice will build these skills into the fingers. Pupils might be cautious about the C♯ minor key but they will hopefully have come to terms with it in their scales and the physical shapes are quite user-friendly.

This is a sensible choice for pupils with small hands, especially if they have a flair for precision. Occasionally, very musical pupils will instinctively shape the right-hand quavers with tiny touches of *rubato*, while keeping the main beats in place. This is wonderful but as rare as this sort of miniature piece in the young pianist's repertoire.

B:6 Glière *Rondo*

By this grade, pupils may be developing an awareness of the structure of pieces. Those of a pragmatic disposition will cheer at the rondo pattern, realizing that the same material recurs, so there are fewer notes to be learned. Cheerful music like this can sound jolly, sprightly and uplifting but, due to the fairly straightforward nature of the theme, could also come over as a touch banal and pedestrian, if not played with enough vitality.

Andantino at around crotchet = 72 seems ideal. A little faster would still succeed musically, providing – and this is the crux of the matter – that the articulation is clear in each hand and the hands are well co-ordinated. Technique and musical conviction go hand in hand and both need to be working equally here. A brisk, fluent performance without shape and colour would be boringly mechanical but a sensitive, musical approach without enough clarity and control would be messy.

The left hand needs as much precision as the right in the accompanying chords and exact rests, and also when it has the melody, or is working in unison with the right hand. Each hand needs to know when to take the limelight and when to retreat a little to allow the other through. Whatever the chosen fingering, it must be consistent and hold up under performance conditions.

The most dramatic changes of colour happen on the second page, with strong, rhythmic *fortes* from bar 24, then a sudden magical change into the *cantabile* at bar 28, where a *piano* would not only highlight the pleasurable shock of the key change but also prepare the way for the following *crescendo* at bar 30.

Technical demands slightly outweigh the interpretative ones, so this is a piece for pupils who have a good finger facility and ability to project a strong rhythm. Certain melodies have a habit of staying on your mind long past the practice time. This could well be one of them.

C:1 Bartók *Harmonics*

This is an intriguing and effective piece from volume 4 of Bartók's six volumes of *Mikrokosmos*. The mysterious sound of the left-hand chords resonating in sympathy with the right-hand tune lends a ghostly atmosphere. The angry *sforzatissimo* chords contrast with the soothing folk melody in the opening but eventually take over and the piece finishes with a roar.

Pupils will delight in experimenting with the sound; this is an effective and attention-grabbing piece and I would anticipate it suiting the more flamboyant extrovert and technically assured, as the ending in particular is quite demanding and requires quick reactions.

No, you haven't got the music upside down, the clefs really are this way up for the first bar and will need to be kept an eye on throughout the piece as they change very frequently. Allow the melody plenty of musical shape and flexibility but otherwise notice that many of the musical considerations are already decided for you in absolute detail as Bartók has hardly left a bar unmarked. For once, take all wedge accents and *sforzatissimo* markings absolutely literally using very active and strong fingers and plenty of arm weight to get the sonority. All the tempo relationships need working out and the *rallentandi* carefully judged. An effective performance will also contrast the *staccato* and *legato* character and all the dynamics.

Pupils will be very eager to practise the 'silent' chords but if you can curb their enthusiasm I would start at the end of the piece, where the athletic right-hand leaps need practising, keeping the tone short and vibrant and checking the accidentals. Practise these chords with the left hand in place, though not necessarily playing anything, so that the pupil gets used to the slightly unnatural sensation of hand crossing at speed.

Finally, those 'silent' chords. Playing these will not necessarily be as easy as it sounds as they often need to be found quickly. The important thing to be aware of is the point at which you feel a faint 'click' as you gently depress the key. This is the point at which the double escapement comes into play but it is harder to feel on an upright piano and is one very good reason for trying out the piano before playing this piece. Any examiner will be only too happy to allow you to do so, so please ask.

C:2 Anthony Herschel Hill *Castles in the Air*

A bluesy, improvisatory little number with luscious chords providing a wonderful harmonic carpet while the right-hand musical gestures give a fairy-tale image to the piece. A dream-like landscape of colours, pointed towers and walking on clouds. The soft, velvety harmonies are only broken once in the middle section as the dreamer almost wakes.

The suggested tempo is relaxed and spacious and will give plenty of time for all those imaginative colours and sounds. This is supported by the *comodo* marking, so no rushing or driving the music forwards, please. Instead, the piece needs a fluidity and flexibility, suiting an imaginative and musical pupil.

Technically, there are few real difficulties, except to achieve the right sound at the appropriate moment. Be careful of the right-hand jumps from the chords to the melodic fragments, which should not begin with an accent. 'Lean' into the first quaver chord of each bar with a relaxed arm and play as *legato* as possible between the chords. These chords need to continue effortlessly through the performance, almost as if played as a duet, with the Primo player simply improvising above.

Very little pedal is marked but clearly much more is needed; indeed, some bars are impossible to play without it. One important point to remember in the pianist's soundworld is that a *staccato* touch with the pedal held down is a very different sound from a more *legato* touch with pedal. In bar 10, for instance, use a finger *staccato* with pedal to achieve a very particular quality to the sound but in bar 11 it should be very *legato* as marked.

Clarify the distribution between the hands at the end and enjoy the rich, colourful harmony of the final three bars.

C:3 Gershwin, arr. Beale *I Got Plenty o' Nuttin'*

Most students will probably be attracted by this arrangement yet, although some will be familiar with many of Gershwin's great melodies, others may know only one or perhaps none. This is a wonderful opportunity to introduce your pupils to Gershwin's accessible and exciting music.

A quick guided tour through *Rhapsody in Blue, An American in Paris* and many of the more famous songs from his musicals will soon encourage a familiarity with the style and, if you get the opportunity, do try to hear Gershwin's own playing taken from piano rolls and available on CD. As a barest minimum, outline the story of *Porgy and Bess* to your pupils and get to know the lyrics of the original song.

Most of the piece needs a relaxed and easy swing and pupils will need to feel instinctively comfortable with all the rhythms and syncopation. Encourage them to improvise on some of the harmonies, using some of the notated rhythms to help inspire a freedom and confidence in their playing. Do take note of the helpful written instructions and phrase markings but interpret them as opportunities, not restrictions; a worked-out rhythmical performance will always sound somewhat mechnical and stilted.

Most of the inherent problems in this piece are stylistic but there are a few tricky moments, such as bars 29 and 37, where a relaxed arm and some slow practice is needed to play the successive chords with ease and to hold the minims. The accidentals and notes will need to be read carefully – the harmonies take a few unexpected directions – and the balance of the parts will need some careful listening. It is surprising how simply balancing the notes in a slightly different way can change the whole character of the piece.

The introduction is improvisatory. Take plenty of time to enjoy the rich harmonies, balancing the chords towards the top and warming them with a touch of pedal. The opening to the song needs an equally relaxed freedom. Allow it a gentle swing, with the tune to the fore and light supporting harmonies. Perhaps give just a touch more tone on the bass notes, as if supported by a double bass.

Don't be afraid to use the pedal in the third line. Even though it isn't marked, it needs it; avoid obscuring the phrasing in the fourth line, though. Instead, enjoy the rhythmic vitality and jokey dissonances.

The middle section ('Swing hard') is much more brassy and rhythmical. Show the rests and imagine you are directing a Big Band, bringing in all the notes (instruments) together and matching the articulation. Make the most of the off-beat accents in bars 29, 34 and 35 and enjoy sliding up those wonderful chromatic swung quaver chords in bar 37.

C:4 Richard Rodney Bennett *Diversion No. 2*

A gentle diversion down an impressionist path is a delightful introduction to a more contemporary style. The sound-world here hints at Debussy and

Benjamin Britten and will be happily entered by most pupils of whatever age. It's always encouraging when the piece is printed on one page. A glance shows that the arpeggios of the opening and final sections flowingly enclose the more firmly rhythmic middle bars, beginning at bar 9.

Although the arpeggios consist entirely of equal semiquavers, musical pupils will feel the natural rise and fall indicated by the *crescendo* and *diminuendo* hairpin signs and will respond to these with a slight increase in momentum to the top, followed by a relaxing balance in the second half of the bar.

Rubato is hard to describe in words but you will have your own ways, gestures, singing and demonstrations to encourage this sensitivity in those who may need to be helped along the way to expressive playing.

Pedalling is helpfully marked. Don't overlook the *simile* sign, which continues until bar 7, where the pedal is held for the whole bar. The middle section, with its semitone triplets, is not pedalled and this adds to the change of colour, making it more cleanly defined.

The musical detail is precisely marked and each small line or hairpin helps the various chords to make their point with a little more emphasis. These signs should be kept in context, as too strong an accent would be out of place. Just a gentle lean on each chord shows the harmony and shape of the moment.

Despite the rippling effect of the semiquavers, the notes must be neatly articulated. Any tendency to leave two or more notes down at a time will need to be watched at an early stage, as old habits die hard.

Through all three sections, a secure basic beat underpins the changes. There may be potential rhythmic errors from bars 9–15 and examiners may hear performances where the triplets are either too fast or too slow. The tied notes could also be cut short, so keep a firm hold of the basic crotchet pulse.

Dynamics are slightly at variance with the look of the piece on the page. The outer sections appear gentler than the apparently more forthright writing of the middle section but this is where the dynamic level is actually at its most subtle.

So much is packed into this single page. Pupils will take to it eagerly and should find that several skills have been painlessly acquired.

C:5 L. Berkeley *Allegro Moderato*

Here you could imagine a French cartoon character walking jauntily along the promenade twirling a stick. Lennox Berkeley's years in France show in this short piece and its wit, rhythmic quirks and clean texture make it an unusual but attractive choice.

Everything is neat and tidy on the page and so it should be in the playing. Crisp fingerwork is needed in the right hand and no less precision, though at a quieter level, for the left hand. These accompanying quavers are more comfortable to play than they look. A slight rocking action from the outside fingers to the thumb keeps the evenness without tension.

The syncopated bars are cheeky but watch the rhythm – plenty of clapping might be necessary to ensure complete accuracy here. Bar 3 will not cause a problem as long as the left hand keeps going in strict time and the right-hand notes slot in exactly with the correct bass quavers.

Dramatic changes of dynamics in the 'terraced' style are very much part of the immediacy of the piece. The super-smooth *legato* phrases at bars 11–16 are a charming surprise and the rude, interrupting quavers, almost like children's gestures, just add to the fun.

Vitality is a precious quality in playing and this piece cannot really succeed without it. Safe fingers are the starting point to bigger issues. It's hopeless trying to convey a jaunty swagger when you're worrying about the next note. Only bars 18–19 present physical difficulties, which may take a little time to respond to slow treatment, but the whole piece does ask for confident finger articulation and irresistible striding rhythm.

For those who choose their three pieces with a view to programme planning, this would make an ideal end to the group. The sunny, slightly Left Bank, atmosphere may need some lively discussion between teacher and pupil, especially if the pupil responds to visual images. This piece could almost be background music to a film and images always help young players to tackle a new style with more conviction.

C:6 Graham Fitkin *SAZZ*

'Plenty of pedal' and 'smooth and relaxed' are friendly instructions and the clarity of appearance of the piece leads to fairly quick assimilation of the notes. Once in the system, this is likely to be exam-proof and ideal for pupils with reasonably sized hands, confident pedalling and an ear for colour. No high-risk passage work here but an ability to coax appropriate sounds out of a possibly unfamiliar exam piano will be one of the considerations.

You may be temporarily puzzled by the double bars but these simply show the composer's thoughtful marking of the changing sections. The melody spans quite long distances at the relaxed pace, so needs clear projection and careful grading of tone.

Listening to the supporting chords, then making the top line sing out more, while still phrasing, will be a fascinating business for some pupils. Others will find the harmonies strange at first, then grow to enjoy them more than they expected.

Only the first bar has a dynamic marking and certainly the whole range of tone is on the subtle side. The section beginning at bar 20 suggests a slightly stronger level and without this rise in tone, the overall structure would be less successful. Quite a few dotted-minim chords fall on the second beats of the bar. These all repeat the harmony of the first beat, so keep them gentle, especially from bars 36–44.

It may be easier to play the upper notes of the bigger bass-clef chords with the right hand, particularly in bars 12–18, remembering that the right-hand outside fingers still need to maintain the *legato* melody. Rhythm should not be a problem but those who are still developing a reliable sense of pulse may have to guard against hurrying on minims in the second half of the bar.

The piece casts its own spell and is likely to be relished by pupils with a strongly individual streak.

GRADE 6

Reaching this grade means that there has been strong motivation and commitment, often at a time when school work has also been more demanding. Reference to the Basis of Assessment printed in *These Music Exams* will show how the musical and stylistic elements need to be part of the performance in order to pass at this level. Most candidates who progress to the later grades do, in fact, show their musicality in its various degrees and stages of development. There is now such a wide variety of choice in the syllabus that the emerging musicianship and individuality of pupils can be encouraged and displayed with suitable material.

LIST A

The Mozart sonata movement will be popular and the Bach 'Allegro in D minor' should suit most players. The Haydn needs stamina and sparkling articulation, which also applies to the Telemann fantasia movement. 'La Lutine' is marginally more challenging than the Bach 'Sinfonia No. 13 in A minor' but has a very clear, intriguing mood.

LIST B

The Satie will be heard many times in the exams and Field's 'Nocturne No. 13 in D minor' and Gounod's 'Prelude in C minor' will also immediately appeal (although larger hands are necessary for the latter). The Moszkowski study and Smetana's 'Souvenir' need independence of hands and musical sensitivity, while the Grieg is lyrical in a light, precise way. This is a charming miniature but would not respond well to a 'driven' approach.

LIST C

Don't be put off by the 5/8 time signature in 'Swedish Caprice'. It needs stamina and buoyancy but, once rhythmically felt, should cause little anxiety. Krenek's 'Glass Figures' depends on stable rhythm and a command of tone colour, while the Norton and Pascal pieces are for the natural jazzers. The Prokofiev needs neat accuracy and an unserious approach and the Bartók is not too difficult technically, provided the preparation is patient and careful attention is paid to all markings.

A:1 J. S. Bach *Sinfonia No.13 in A minor*

'It's time Wilhelm Christian got down to some serious practice!' Bach wrote this three-part sinfonia for his eldest son, 'to foster a *cantabile* style of playing', and this short piece probably caused even a member of the Bach family to do some slow, careful work.

The part-playing is the main consideration and pupils will need a good left-hand technique and ability to define each line cleanly, at a one-in-a-bar tempo. Look first at bars 36–40 when deciding on a tempo, as the demisemiquavers here could cause the impetus to slacken if too optimistic a speed has been chosen. This is also the passage where neat articulation might lose its edge if the fingers are too relaxed. When this section has been mastered, practise matching the tempo to the opening three bars, avoiding the all-too-tempting trap of playing the easier bars too quickly.

Examiners quite frequently hear performances in which the tempo of a piece fluctuates depending on the ease or difficulty of the notes in each phrase. The ability to keep a regular basic pulse is a crucial skill which needs to be acquired as early as possible. Even at the early stages of the Preparatory Test we can hear immediately the fortunate, well-taught youngsters who are aware of this feeling – and it is a feeling, not something that one *thinks*.

Having sorted out the general approach and avoided some common pitfalls, the next step is practice at a slow enough tempo to settle fingering, articulation and touch. As we know that Bach was aiming this piece at his son's *cantabile* playing, we obviously continue this *legato*, singing tone into the semiquavers after the opening three bars. The tempo and style are unsuitable for a full-blown Romantic sound but a smooth, singing tone could still be kept in mind. You may decide to detach the left-hand quavers or keep these *legato* as well. Both approaches work successfully.

As there is so much going on in the three parts, keep an awareness of the graceful one-in-a-bar feeling as work progresses, otherwise concentration on fingering and neat semiquavers could cause that unintentionally mechanical effect which professionals rudely but aptly call 'typewriting'.

Once again the ornaments add extra polish but could be left out or simplified. Those printed over bars 3 and 7 might be too elaborate for most pupils and could hold up the flow. Neat mordents starting on the beat would be a sensible compromise. The fingering suggestions work well and also help to avoid bumps at larger intervals, which could stick out after the scale patterns.

Pupils often learn to listen to the right hand first and take longer to separate their awareness of any additional lines. Practising each part in isolation will help this process, which is sometimes felt to be a bore by youngsters in a hurry but is a necessary aspect of all good piano playing.

Setting specific goals for certain kinds of work helps, such as 'Practise bars 8–24 with each part separately, then hands together at this (slow) speed', and will produce better results than, 'Learn up to here and do some separate practice'.

The natural rise and fall of the lines, plus the harmonic structure, tend to shape the music without 'putting in' dynamics. It is often sensible in this style to simply mark the quieter places and main climaxes of sections, then let things unfold from the starting points. For instance, a *mezzo piano* opening, rising a little to bar 7, then another quieter start at bar 8 gives the pattern. In general the cadences show the most positive moments and the bars following them drop down in preparation for the gradual rise to the next main point.

It is likely that even Wilhelm Christian had his problem bars on the way to mastering this piece and his father probably had to exercise the same mixture of determination and patience that modern teachers need to see work through to a successful conclusion.

A:2 F. Couperin *La Lutine*

Most pupils scarcely glance at scholarly footnotes, wanting to get on with the music. Teachers reading through the notes will find this illuminating quote from Wilfred Mellers' book on Couperin, which provides a vital clue to this piece:

A little piece about sprites and goblins such as were rampant in bacchanalian revels in masques and divertissements.

Mellers continues:

Though the limits of decorum should be preserved, one should, in playing this piece, emphasize the angularities of the theme in slightly uncomfortable grotesquerie.

The alliance of gleeful demonic energy and controlled, neat fingerwork may seem a bit unlikely in many pupils and it will take well-planned, patient work to put in the necessary foundation before the sprites and goblins can make their appearance.

The quaver chord at the end of the first main section reveals the reason for the disconcerting five quavers in the first bar. In order to catch the vitality of the opening, try a quick intake of breath to set up the rhythm, as a tame start will kill the mood.

On an early keyboard instrument it would be much easier to incorporate the ornaments, even at a very lively tempo, and we should not sacrifice speed and impact for the sake of embellishments, which are demanding at this grade, especially in the left hand. Neat mordents at cadence points will still make the point and the footnotes state: 'For the purposes of the exam, ornaments in round brackets can be omitted without penalty.' Examiners know what can be reasonably expected at each grade and assess the performance as a whole, rather than taking off marks for one aspect which in any case is a matter of personal taste.

Staccato quavers help the texture and energy of the piece more than a *legato* bass and there are some quite wide leaps which have to be managed up to speed. Watch the left-hand rests – these need to be exact, as does the part playing where held notes sustain the line.

Precision and vitality are the key words, coupled with a light but clean attack. Examiners sometimes hear over-enthusiastic articulation in this kind of piece with every semiquaver hammered out like machine-gun fire. Whilst respecting the physical agility and strength it takes to achieve this, they will undoubtedly mention the lack of shape such an approach produces, as the musical fluctuations and lighter beats are lost in the excessive articulation. A finger touch works best, keeping the dance lilt and enjoying the quirks of the hemiolas, when square brackets show the rhythmic subtleties. This feature actually works perfectly well, whether it is intellectually understood or not. Just play the notes rhythmically and Couperin does the rest.

Some dynamic planning of an unfussy kind always adds to the structure in performance and we are given a free hand in this piece. Decide first where each section comes to its main point, then build towards these moments. The end of the first section could be the first dynamic destination, then the cadence at bars 15–16. These resolutions might be followed by quieter starts, giving contrast and a chance to build towards the next climax. The second half culminates at the more emphatic bars 30–31 which, as repeats are not required, lead straight to the final bar.

Independence of hands is vital for a successful performance and so is an invigorating two-in-a-bar, maintained evenly through the various technical hurdles.

Despite all the semiquavers, this all lies quite comfortably under the hands, even though they are sometimes quite far apart on the keyboard. Quick glances at the left hand may be necessary, adding to the safety level, provided that the pupil also immediately looks up again at the page. This kind of piece is difficult to restart or rescue after an accident, so aim for rock-like stability.

Experiencing the sound and feel of the early instrument makes all the difference when performing keyboard music of this period. Once experienced in the ears and fingers, it makes a lasting impression. Purists may shudder but I have found that one sheet of newspaper laid over the strings of a grand piano for a few moments' playing will give the pupil something of the feel of the original. Besides, it's another way to make the lesson fun and memorable.

A:3 Mozart *Allegro*

This could be called an early work but the age of 18 or 19 in Mozart's case is probably the equivalent of about 45 to the rest of us. It is significant that this is the last movement of the sonata and it has a bright, positive mood but with all the subtle lyricism one would expect, even if these qualities make only brief but telling appearances. This is slightly less physically demanding than either the Bach or Couperin but it needs more musical insight from the player.

The phrasing falls into predictable four-bar patterns but it is less visually obvious where the all-important main points lie. Your ears will tell you more than your eyes and, on playing through, teachers will pick up the gentle emphasis needed on the first beats of bars 4 and 8, the typical 'feminine endings' which immediately show the graceful style of the period. Similar opportunities occur throughout but Mozart is never predictable and only playing the piece will reveal the shapes.

The tonal contrasts are boldly marked *piano* and *forte* on the page and certainly need clear projection but the quieter levels must avoid flimsiness and the louder bars should never be harsh. Musical pupils will naturally respond to the *legato* lyrical phrases starting at bars 16 and 24 in the first main section and will be equally expressive – but with no loss of tempo – when similar patterns occur later. The arpeggiated chords are rather like a harpsichord in effect: fast and rhythmically incisive for emphasis, not romantically spread for colour.

Teachers often worry about pedalling in Mozart. The concern is: some or none? It is quite possible to give a tonally satisfying performance without using any pedal but little touches to enhance lyrical corners or aid *legato* would be used by most experienced players. Pupils who have 'discovered' *legato* pedalling sometimes tend to use it all the time without being aware of the smudging of detail and quick harmonic changes in the bar that too liberal an application will cause. If you like the effect, a touch on the first beats of bars 10 and 12 will help the E♭s to sing but holding the pedal right through the bars will sound too Romantic in texture. As with fingering, the only realistic answer is to try various options and find out what succeeds. This concentration on listening and deciding is much more educationally sound than simply following someone else's suggestions.

Detail is important. Exact length of notes, slurs, detached notes, balance of hands (especially when the left hand has semiquavers) all give inflection and character to the playing. By this grade examiners hope that candidates, as well as managing the notes at a suitable tempo, will also make each piece sound as if it has been written by its own composer. We quite often hear Mozart played with the luxurious sonorities of Brahms and Brahms performed with a dryness more appropriate to early music. Finding the right tone colour is a fascinating pursuit and some guidance at an early stage of a new piece will prevent pupils working with too heavy or flimsy a physical approach for a whole week. It is just as easy for the finger memory to latch onto the right feel, as it is to remember a less stylish level.

The tempo needs to be brisk but not frantic and some of the suggested ornaments are fun to incorporate. The upbeat turn on the F of bar 9 is elegant, providing the following E♭ stays safely in place, and this could apply to bar 11 but a final turn in bar 12 is less advisable, as the following semiquavers need to start rhythmically. The appoggiaturas at bars 3, 31 and 34 simply become four even semiquavers.

Most of the more introverted material happens in the middle section from bar 40 and, again, tone colour will convey a sensitive response to this interlude. When the opening theme returns at bar 62, the phrasing mirrors its first appearance but the turn on the B♭ in bar 70 is not as comfortable as in its previous incarnation and might unsettle the interval of a seventh on black keys. In the heat of the moment practicality and safety win every time over aesthetic considerations, so if this is a problem, go for the reliable option and leave it out each time.

At face value this is uncomplicated, breezy music with manageable technical challenges but sensitive pupils will be aware of the undertones that are never far beneath the surface. Musical maturity arrives in its own time and many candidates will be playing this movement at the same age as Mozart composed it.

A:4 J. C. F. Bach *Allegro in D minor*

Johann Christoph Friedrich Bach was the sixteenth of J. S. Bach's 20 children and possibly the first to write 'for Harpsichord or Pianoforte' on the title page of a sonata, although this piece is still much more harpsichord-orientated and needs suitable clarity of articulation. It has a simple cheerfulness, elegance and charm, which becomes more evident if you imagine two singers or instrumentalists performing it as a duet.

The piece shouldn't present too many technical problems once the fingering is learnt and control of the semiquavers and ornaments is mastered. Practise the semiquaver passages in varying rhythms and with gentle off-beat accents to help gain the control, thus giving them essential vibrancy and clarity. Treat the ornaments as an integral part of the melodic line to avoid panic; keep them light and give them musical direction.

One or two small sections may prove a little awkward for some. The left-hand entries in bars 11 and 12 could well come in late and need some careful work. Pupils may also need to be encouraged to lift their hands for the all-important rests and may need to be reminded that these not only provide the performer with time to get the hands ready but also add to the rhythmic energy.

It is the character of each of the two parts, however, and their inter-action, that provide the main challenges. Make sure the hands know exactly where they are going separately, including the shape and phrasing, then put them gracefully together. This is an excellent piece to practise as a duet; at no point do the hands interfere with one another, so teacher and pupil can explore the musical subtleties together.

The editorial dynamics are a good starting point and will help the pupil understand the architecture of the piece. It essentially falls into two halves (bars 1–18 and 18 to the end) both of which rise to a top B♭ and then descend. Know where the various sequences are going so that you don't arrive at your maximum dynamic too soon and always remember to come down again to give scope for later *crescendi*.

Experiment with the phrasing to give the piece buoyancy but don't forget to point out the jazzy syncopation in bars 1–4 and 7–10, gently separating the first note. It may prove a valuable way in to the character of the piece for some pupils.

A:5 Haydn *Allegro*

This allegro is Haydn at his most humorous and jovial; it is full of teasing, mimicked laughter, false trails and smiles. Many pupils will be attracted to the piece because of its ready appeal but they may also relish the fact that they are learning a whole and substantial sonata movement. You might even suggest the possibility of learning the whole sonata for a performance.

Stamina and good concentration are essential attributes for a successful performance, along with an athletic finger agility and sparkling articulation.

This is a second movement and essentially in rounded binary form. Some discussion about the structure of the movement could form part of the initial preparation. The second section (really a development) leads us swiftly through large numbers of keys as if teasing us with false entries and the possible return of the opening before the real thing in bar 89. Even here Haydn has to have his little joke, leading us astray in bars 90 to 97 only to arrive in bar 98 exactly where we expected to be.

Typically, Haydn gives a little time for the fingers to warm up before throwing some more demanding passage-work in front of the player. The couplets in the right hand (bar 36) need a relaxed wrist and the groups of six and the demisemiquavers in bars 44 and 48 should be light and agile despite the *forte* marking. In fact the large number of notes will make the dynamic for you – the important thing is not to labour the pulse, so do check the tempo occasionally with a metronome.

The left hand needs a bassoon-like *staccato* on the quavers, not too spiky, but bouncy. The right-hand needs short up-beat quavers and then to 'lean' gently into the first semiquaver of the opening phrase, keeping the final quaver short but not accented.

Make the most of the slightly rude dissonance in bars 28–30 and the hyena-like laughter which follows in bar 34, keeping the grace notes light and close to the main note.

Use dabs of pedal very occasionally to enhance the phrasing and tone but, in general, virtually none is needed and too much would make the piece sound a little woolly.

A:6 Telemann *Allegro*

'Fantasia' derives from the Italian word meaning 'fancy' and the character is generally that of a free improvisation. This is in the Italian style and by one of the most prolific composers ever. The allegro has a horse-riding 'tally-ho' feel to it and, once set in motion, there is no stopping the galloping triplets. It will suit a pupil with athletic fingers, confidence and an instinctive flair and lightness of touch.

If you are using an Urtext or 'clean' edition, then bear in mind that the dotted quaver–semiquaver rhythms in the left hand fall in line with the triplets. If using the suggested edition, you will notice that the piece is punctuated with commas. These are an opportunity for taking a short breath and for lifting the hands but not for stopping the gallop, so avoid taking time.

Apart from the stamina to cope with the almost continuous triplets, there is in fact little to concern the pupil technically once the fingers have learnt the notes. There are a few awkward hand positions to get used to but hands can generally be phrased together and there is plenty of time for the few small mordents, as long as they are kept light.

Telemann's own suggested phrasing in the first two bars gives the piece excellent rhythmic drive and will give you a good idea of the style and character to achieve. Aim for a flamboyant and positive start, lightening the fourth beats and the second and third notes of each group of quavers.

Contrast the delightful sequence in bars 5 to 7 with the opening and experiment with the phrasing of the left-hand crotchets, perhaps keeping them gently detached in bars 8 and 9 and *legato* (as marked in the recommended edition) for bars 10 and 11. The same applies to bars 38–41.

Any suggested dynamics are an excellent starting point. Try them out and then experiment with your own but use them to highlight the structure of the piece, guiding the listener through the various sections. There are plenty of opportunities to change the colour. Treat it like an interesting and varied conversation with a variety of different moods. The most important thing to bear in mind is that the texture is quite thin and the piece needs to remain on its toes, so grade the *crescendi* carefully or the tone will become too heavy.

B:1 Field *Nocturne No.13 in D minor*

A distinguished teacher always leaves a lasting mark and John Field's early studies with Clementi can be seen, if not so much heard. The Alberti bass and classical appearance of the main theme are very familiar features of the earlier era. The harmonies and warmly expressive melody are another matter and lean towards Chopin, who was anticipated by the Irishman John Field by some 20 years.

The way to the heart of this piece is to combine the neat clarity of Clementi with the *rubato* and *cantabile* of Chopin. One without the other would not really hit the stylistic target. *Lento plaintivo* and the D minor key create a gentle melancholy but this is not a tragedy and crotchet = 80 is an important direction to give the necessary flow.

This will strongly appeal to sensitive, expressive pupils but may also reveal unexpected depths in pupils who usually seem more at home with pop music. Teaching the first group will be a matter of encouraging their natural tendencies, whilst the second category will probably require explanation and demonstration of *rubato*.

Phrasing in this early Romantic piece needs good awareness and planning of *rubato*. Too much and it will be seasick and sentimental, none or too little will be boring and matter-of-fact. Identify the main points of the first few phrases – perhaps the first beats of bars 3, 7 and 12 – then practise increasing the momentum evenly and gently towards these points. This will create the time to linger affectionately at the moments that need emphasis. Picking up the tempo immediately afterwards is vital to get the next phrase on the way and keep the overall structure intact. Pupils are usually more inclined to linger than to move on; the latter takes more musical conviction but both ebb and flow are equally important.

Pedalling is quite an issue here. *Legato* pedalling should be safely established by this grade and it will be needed throughout but with extra care in certain passages. The demisemiquavers in bars 42–43 and the dotted semiquavers from bars 52–54 will need either no pedal, or frequent, skilful changes for those with advanced co-ordination between foot and ear. Otherwise, change with the harmonies, watching the left hand care-fully, as sometimes two or three changes will be needed per bar. The semi-tones from bars 12–14 and similar passages will also need special care to avoid running into one another.

The *più moto* is quite declamatory and certainly needs some freedom and bolder shaping. The agitated syncopation and left-hand leaps all add drama. Make sure the drama is in the musical mood and not in physical accidents here, as the left hand needs a good aim for these thirds, which have quite firm emphasis on the first of each pair.

Where accents are marked *sforzando*, the tone is still *cantabile* and beautiful. These could be misunderstood and become too heavy. Throughout the piece, the theme has three quavers before the first main beat, leading the theme across the bar line. Careful grading of tone will be needed, otherwise the first quaver could be too heavy, unsettling the rhythm.

In every set of three exam pieces, pupils usually secretly or openly have a favourite. This is likely to be the one for many candidates and the enjoyment of the music will carry them through the early stages of Romantic playing.

B:2 Moszkowski *Study in G minor*

The first question to ask when beginning work on a study is 'What's it for?' It's a great help to know which aspect of the playing is under scrutiny and will hopefully be improved. In the case of this charming melodic study, there is not a semiquaver in sight and no sign of the usual velocity trials. Something less obvious is the aim here, which will need just as much awareness to achieve as high-speed flourishes.

The expressive melody is simply but beautifully constructed and is supported by an equally economical bass line. In between, however, is a weaving pattern of quavers, continuously filling in the harmonies with extra passing notes. Keeping the busiest line in the background, while projecting melody and bass, always with care for balance, is the objective. Examiners often refer to 'balance of hands', especially in the early grades, simply meaning the relative levels of melody and accompaniment but here both hands are involved with the quaver background, so the sounds must also match from one hand to the other.

It is up to the performer to decide in which places the quavers can be more comfortably taken by the left hand but start by considering bars 2 and 6, from the third quavers, which also explains the suggested finger change on the bass D – an organist's trick, often used to keep the sound sustained. Pianists tend to rely heavily on the pedal but a combination of finger connection plus sensitive pedalling achieves the best result.

Examiners will hope to hear three smoothly maintained lines: a *cantabile* melody, carefully judged quavers and a warm, sustained bass line. Each part contributes to the phrasing, which is quite romantic but often culminates in 'feminine' endings, such as at bar 4, when the minim G is stronger than the following F♯. There needs to be room to breathe between phrases but keep the underlying momentum, as this is just another form of *rubato*, which adds expression but does not interrupt the overall shape.

The three main sections each have some repetition and dynamics are given but at each level there is also a natural rise and fall, helped by the nature of the writing. The rising sequence from bar 13–16 helps to emphasize the top G but too soon a *crescendo* will make the second G hard to achieve with a *cantabile* tone. The following *diminuendo* is also best delayed, so that a really effective *piano*, with perhaps a little easing of tempo, introduces the return of the first melody.

Problems may occur with the intrusive quavers, breaks in the *legato* melody and bass notes released too soon. A daunting list but the lovely melody sweetens the pill and most studies are written to improve an aspect of technique, so the hurdles are there for a good reason. Having a clear idea of the musical priorities puts things in proportion and a few non-*legato* quavers are not disastrous if melody and bass are sustained and the pedal thoughtfully used. Practising only the outer lines will help pupils listen for the potential breaks in the line, which can then be more knowingly joined when the quavers are introduced to complete the texture.

Giving the impression of ease is a sign of real mastery. Be sure that the pedal is released carefully in the last bar and that the final octave is rhythmically posed, as it would be all too easy to cut short the previous bar in the relief of having safely arrived.

B:3 Satie *Gymnopédie No.1*

It can't be easy to be a composition student at the same time as Debussy and it is only in recent years that Satie's piano pieces have caught the popular taste. Many pupils will have heard this irresistibly world-weary piece and its appeal is immediate.

Lent and *douloureux* give a more funereal impression than the music really creates; it is based on a slow dance, so the downbeat mood should not be overstated. Much of Satie's music seems to have one foot in a Montmartre night club and seeing a poster of one of the famous Toulouse-Lautrec paintings will help present-day youngsters to get a feel for the idiom.

Those who still shy away from *legato* pedalling should avoid this choice, as continuous pedalling, catching the low dotted minim each bar, is essential for the authentic tone colour. Make sure the pedal is down before these notes are released, otherwise the foundation of the bar is lost.

The middle line of chords gives the rest of the harmonic picture, so stay below the dynamic level of the right-hand melody. The distances for the left hand to cover are quite wide. Pupils will help accuracy by looking at the keys and having most of the left hand memorized. Moving quickly between the single low notes and the chords is a knack that may take some encouragement. It is more usual for the physical movement to be made at the same sort of tempo as the piece but experienced players cover the distances much more quickly, giving themselves time to prepare the notes before they are needed. The hypnotic pulse will be the starting point of a convincing performance. Uneven or missing beats will show up and one slip could spoil the rest.

It is no accident that I have considered the melody after the rest of the texture. Expressive and languorous as it is, the chords below set the scene, so are better established before the right-hand crotchets are shaped into phrases. Some of the chords, or parts of them, are more comfortably taken by the right hand and these have been indicated by square brackets.

The geographical distances between the hands are quite large at times and it will help to keep a visual overview of the entire span, rather than concentrating on one line. It's surprising how much of the keyboard is included in the peripheral vision once pupils become aware of it.

Although dynamics range from *piano* to *forte*, all sounds are gently sonorous and the loudest part, around bar 48, is in proportion to the introverted level of the rest. Matching a *cantabile*, *legato* line constructed in even crotchets, without unevenness of tone or rhythm is quite demanding. Concentrated listening will be an ingredient in every performance and this kind of exposed writing is harder on an unfamiliar piano. Better to play the scales and at least one other piece first in the exam, before embarking on this appealing miniature, with its unmistakable *tristesse*.

B:4 Gounod *Prelude in C minor*

This prelude is a soulful and elegiac melody from a French master of song writing. In fact, think of it as a song without words with the introduction (bars 1–9) a sweeping and impassioned musical arch, such as might link a recitative with an aria. The song (bars 11–30) is a repeated soulful melody over gentle, throbbing chords, followed by the final few mournful bars. It will suit a reflective and serious musician with a fairly large hand as one or two passages are a lot easier if they can be comfortably stretched.

Technically, the opening is the most demanding part, as it needs to be projected and elegantly shaped. Imagine it as if performed by different instruments in the string section of an orchestra, each previous entry beautifully phrased-off under the beginning of the next entry. The lines need to be *legato* at all times and notes must be lifted at the appropriate time to clarify the texture. Pedalling will need to be carefully judged, perhaps with a dab of pedal on the opening octave and then at the beginning of each bar.

A small *ritardando* in bars 7 to 8 will ease the way into the opening of the song in bar 9. Here the tone on the chords needs to be very carefully chosen and controlled. A little more on the first two but thereafter, once the strings have begun to vibrate, they will need to become even softer to avoid becoming too intrusive. The pedal and notes are straightforward.

The trill in bar 20 should start on the note, two groups of four then a group of five, with a turn. The sixths in bars 27 and 28 will need to be absolutely *legato* and the substitution will work well here, although you might prefer to put 4/1 on the fourth chord of bar 27, then 3/1 substituting to 5/1 on the next. If the hand is big enough, hold the bottom G in bar 29 to enable the pedal changes without losing the harmony.

Musically, the melody may seem a little repetitive but use this as an opportunity to explore with your pupils the many ways they might say or sing the same phrase depending on their mood and meaning. 'This is my destiny' fits well with each phrase, for example, and a new and unique colour could be used for each to give a slightly different emphasis.

Gounod himself has allowed the song to fade away into the lonely distance with a descending bass line and long rests in the right hand. A small *ritardando* at the end will add to the poignancy, as will holding that last chord for its full length plus the quaver rest before allowing the audience to move a muscle.

B:5 Grieg *Vöglein*

The excellent editorial notes and Grieg's title sum up everything you need to know about the background to this piece and the music speaks for itself. It needs lightness, charm, beauty and the 'aaaaah!' factor.

A successful performance will require enormous subtlety of colour and light, even articulation of all demisemiquavers to achieve a 'chirruping' effect. Any unease or lack of control will be only too apparent but, if these are overcome, then the piece almost plays itself, providing the hands jump reasonably quickly to prepare the notes and the sound for the next phrase.

Keep the hands very light and note where Grieg has placed the accent. Then try some slow-performance practice, controlling the sound and shape exactly as when playing fast; make a small *crescendo* through the upbeat demisemiquavers and add just a little extra brightness on the accented first quaver of the next bar, or the other way around later on in the piece, where the accent appears on the first demisemiquaver of the group.

The hands will have to practise a quick jump to cover the notes for the next phrase but must arrive early enough to rest on the surface and avoid an accent on the first note. This will also be true of the arpeggio figures (bars 21, 22, 24, 25), where they will need to cover the whole group of notes in advance for absolute freedom and security.

The phrasing and pedalling is detailed and must be taken literally as it will give the piece its charm. All *staccato* notes must be short and played with a little brightness if accented. Any laziness in the sound here (even if the note is caught with the pedal) will soon cause the performance to lose its sparkle. The pedalling in general is very effective. Try it out conscientiously before experimenting with further use, keeping the up-beat 'chirrups' in bars 6, 7 etc free from pedal as marked to show the phrasing.

The tempo marking may be a little too fast for some instruments. A slightly less frantic tempo (dotted crotchet = 80) will be quite fast enough and allow just that little flexibility and ease. Dynamics are generally soft but leave yourself scope for the *molto pianissimo* at the end as the bird flies away into the distance.

B:6 Smetana *Souvenir*

Most of Smetana's income in his five years in Sweden initially came from piano teaching so it is quite likely that this piece was composed for pupils to play. Whether Smetana's 'Souvenir' came from his native Hungary, or whether it was, as is more likely, a musical souvenir or musical memory is for you to decide. What is certain is that this intensely personal music needs spaciousness and musical sincerity.

As Smetana was a composer of numerous operas, you might think of the tune as a song, perhaps with a cello enhancing the bass line, occasionally taking over the tune as in bars 21–24. The performance will need plenty of pedal and warmth with a well-projected melody.

A sensitive performer will take time over the ornaments and demisemiquavers, preventing them from sounding rushed and merely decorative. Instead they must be melodic. An instinctively musical performer will naturally linger over the top of the second phrase, for instance, and want to take a bit more time in bars 18 and 22.

The left-hand semiquavers require a natural flexibility; don't allow them to 'beat time' or drive the music forwards. The piece needs lots of gentle *rubato*, so the accompaniment must subtly enhance the musical direction of the right-hand melody. A good way of developing the musical *rubato* would be to play the piece as a duet: the teacher playing the tune and deliberately taking plenty of time around corners, the pupil learning to accommodate the accompaniment sensitively around the melody.

Practise the piece without pedal and hold all the bottom left-hand notes as marked to enhance the harmonies. The pedal, when added, should simply colour the performance. Change the pedal with the change of harmonies but in general this will be on every minim or crotchet beat.

Grade the dynamics carefully and shape each musical phrase as beautifully and sensitively as possible, taking note of Smetana's own hairpin markings. Enjoy every nuance of a most beautiful piece of music.

C:1 Christopher Norton *Prelude IV*

An effective and, I suspect, popular jazz prelude, but if your pupil has a weak sense of rhythm then choose it with caution. The detail will give a good, clean performance but it also needs a natural jazz flexibility and sense of improvisation. Suggest some jazz listening to the pupil if they are unfamiliar with the idiom and consider exploring some of the other excellent jazz and rock preludes by the same composer.

The piece divides into three main sections and is technically fairly straightforward. The grace note in bar 1 can be cleanly executed in a 2-1 fingering on the lower notes; 2-3 is just a little unpredictable. The jumps in the right hand (bars 6–7, 34–35 etc) need to be unpanicked and effortless (some 'shadow jumping' might help here) and the chords just before the middle section mustn't sound too percussive; keep a relaxed wrist here.

The main problems are rhythmical. Counting rigorously in quavers will produce a laboured and stilted performance; it needs a strong crotchet pulse throughout the syncopated bars, but this is not easy in bars 4 and 12 and particularly awkward throughout bars 17–19, 41–44, which are real brain teasers and a challenge of co-ordination. Conquer these bars first, encouraging plenty of slow practice until they become innate.

The overall mood of the piece is fairly relaxed, so avoid the tone becoming too heavy and the tempo too energetic; the metronome marking is a good guide. Use a broad range of dynamic colour, balancing the 6ths carefully to avoid a thick texture and joining the top notes with the fingers (where possible) to allow the phrasing some freedom from the excellent pedal markings. Perhaps explore further subtle use of the pedal in the outer sections to enhance the phrasing, being careful not to obscure the rests (as in bar 1). The middle section (bars 27–40) needs to be quite atmospheric and dreamy. Why not bring out the inner line just to add a bit more interest?

C:2 Prokofiev *Cortège de Sauterelles*

To non-French speakers, a quick glance in a French dictionary will pay dividends. *Cortège* is a word sometimes associated with funerals but here the procession is a lively one, comprising grasshoppers. Musical jokes always release performing inhibitions and nervous energy can be productively focused towards the spiky rhythm, which is the essential element throughout.

Articulation needs to be light and crisp in the first and last sections but very obviously contrasted for the *legato* middle part, which starts *poco meno mosso* at bar 16.

There are quite large distances for the left hand to cover from bars 33–40 and the low B must be a bull's-eye every time. Finding this note from the upper octave will secure this corner and shorten the gap. A useful trick is simply to shape the octave Bs but only play the lower one. A little pedal would help this passage but it could equally well be played without, providing the right-hand *legato* is well established.

The various accents are humorous, not aggressive, and although the dynamics have louder moments, grasshoppers are light insects, so a bright sound is a better aim as loudness without imaginative colour could be too heavy or harsh.

The rests are an important feature. Orchestral players are accustomed to giving all these details exact precision but pianists are often less watchful. In fairness to all keyboard players, they do have many more notes at a time to manage than any other instrument and it is no wonder that rests sometimes seem the least of their concerns.

The tempo suggestion is ideal and the *poco meno mosso* only a little less lively. This is a wisp of a piece that will be very successful in the hands of candidates with a well-developed rhythmic sense and inner vitality. The former can be established and helped with skilful teaching but the latter is born rather than bred.

From the *a tempo*, it's best if strict time is kept right to the final bar. A cautionary word may be necessary to make sure this little procession does not run away out of control.

C:3 Ernst Krenek *Glass Figures*

Practical teachers will not pass this one by without further investigation. Although the idiom may be unfamiliar and may take further acquaintance before players feel relaxed about tackling the style, there are at least three advantages to this choice. It is only 23 bars long, so from bar 1 the end is in sight. The musical instructions are very detailed, leaving no doubts as to what the composer wants and, once mastered, the piece will be exam proof, standing up well to performance nerves, as there are no real fluency challenges.

The big proviso is the rhythm. Absolutely solid counting holds the piece in shape. Without it, the fragmentary nature of the writing would be meaningless. Pupils whose sense of basic pulse falters when notes are tricky are better directed to other choices. The rests are also a vital part of the rhythm and clipped silent beats may be a problem for many players, especially where there is no melodic thread.

Contrasts of dynamics and colour – the two are not necessarily the same – are the means of illuminating these glass figures. The sparkle and brilliance of light through glass gives the idea of the sound quality, which the composer asks us to project with clarity at extremes of dynamic level, from *pianissimo* to *fortissimo*. *Molto staccato*, an unusual instruction, gives the colour and touch at the opening, then this melts into *dolce legato* at bars 6 and 7, only to make a brief return at the *a tempo* bar 8.

The climax of the piece is at bars 13 and 14, where a brilliant impact can be made, providing the attack is not too heavy. This should be an exciting moment, not startling the listener for the wrong reasons. A good finger *legato* will be a necessity, as pedal is best avoided, except for those with deft co-ordination and alert ears during bars 10–12. Most candidates will play the entire piece without pedal and this is an ideal chance to explore different forms of finger articulation, all with precision and rhythmic discipline. These sound rather daunting words but, in achieving these different techniques, pupils will be enlivening their palette of colours.

As so often in strange idioms, a mental picture is invaluable in getting under the skin of the piece. If there are no glass figures to hand, try holding up an ice cube to the light and turning it round to see the effect this produces visually; this should influence the pupil's approach to the piece.

C:4 Bartók *Village Joke*

The music gives the impression that the joke here is not a particularly subtle one. Sounds of rather undisciplined 'um-pah' bands and chirpy laughter conjure up images of a rustic and bawdy village fair where farm hands push each other playfully and boisterously into mud-filled ponds. Even the *pesante* marking at the beginning is open to mis-interpretation!

Technically, the piece is not too demanding. 'Abergavenny' fits the groups of five notes rather well to help with the rhythm and the quaver fits exactly mid-way between the 3rd and 4th notes. Check the clefs carefully and don't be put off by the rather uncommon notation in bar 27; simply play all the notes together. The right-hand chords in the seventh line will need memorizing. All the notes are played together despite their appearance and playing the initial two-note chord with the thumb only will help the stretch to the top.

The main difficulty will be checking and familiarizing yourself with all the notes, particularly for the final page, where they become less predictable. Learn each hand separately, making absolutely sure that the fingering chosen is consistent and well-rehearsed to avoid potential accidents under pressure. The left-hand/right-hand co-ordination in bars 15 onwards will need a little slow work initially, while getting used to the independence of the hands.

The character of the piece will require robust left-hand *staccato* with well-graded and contrasted dynamics. A short, crisp *staccato* on all the minor 2nds and chords will keep the piece wide-eyed and alive. There is virtually no call for pedal – just some lively and confident finger work, a broad range of colour and a good deal of coarse humour.

C:5 Claude Pascal *Rose des sables*

This is a smoochy little number reminiscent of Billy Mayerl (as is the flowery title which actually means 'Gypsum Flower'), and if you or your pupil haven't explored any of Mayerl's music, then now is definitely the time to try.

This piece will need an instinctive feel for the flexibility of swing rhythm and those well acquainted with the style will want to swing all the quavers and dotted rhythms – but be careful on the third page; the quavers deliberately grouped in four cry out for more equal treatment. If you are unsure about the swing rhythm, then think in triplets almost throughout and you won't be far wrong – though a more subtle performance will distinguish between the opening and the performance of the quavers in the main melody, which are slightly lazier.

The tempi are very appropriate, but interpret the dotted line as the beginning of the new, slower tempo – the previous crotchet rest is quite long, as it marks the end of the previous *ritardando*.

One of the most common obstacles to a successful performance of this piece will be an obtrusive and rather heavy left hand. Give a little more weight and time on the bass notes and a light lift on the chords as the hand travels back down, almost thinking of the left hand as moving in an anti-clockwise circle. You would be wise to learn at least the bass notes from memory.

The right-hand tune needs to be subtly shaped, be very *legato* and to have a rather seductive *rubato* yet naïve simplicity, if this doesn't sound too contradictory. The frequent right-hand crotchet triplets will need to be relaxed and natural, so put some words with these to help space them out and shape them (using the word '*marsh*mallow' works quite well) and add the left-hand chord gently.

Pedal on beats 1 and 3 but leave it out at those magic moments when the first initial idea returns (bar 13 for instance). Here the right hand will want to savour the quavers after a little breath just before the third beat. The performance will naturally move on to bar 21 and then once again ease its way into the main theme.

Technically there are a few tricky corners where an occasional glance at the hands will be necessary, so learn as much from memory as you can and practise using rests to get the hands into position. Otherwise it is simply a matter of familiarizing yourself with the notes of an enjoyable piece with plenty of sentimentality and subtlety.

C:6 Howard Skempton *Swedish Caprice*

Those pupils familiar with 'Take Five', Dave Brubeck's famous hit, will have mastered the rhythm here already. Once this is done it is simply a matter of learning the order of a few notes. Don't be fooled by the look of the piece or the five flats; it may seem like one of those mind-bending puzzles but all becomes crystal clear once you've got beyond the first eight bars, which present the most rhythmically confusing section. After this the rhythm is much more straightforward and you will soon realize that many of the passages are played again later in the piece. Spot them and you will notice how little there actually is to learn.

This is minimalist music; the interest relies on pointing out the small variations of the patterns. Do this unobtrusively but communicate them to the listener, and explore some Steve Reich or Philip Glass as an introduction to the style. Michael Nyman's music from *The Piano* would also be a good comparison.

Learn the first eight bars last. This may seem a strange option but they become so much easier to play once the feeling of five beats in a bar is instinctive. Until this is the case, the final quaver rest of bars 1 and 3 may well cause a few brains to spin and is not helped by the 2/4 bar at the end of the section.

Take the composer's one dynamic marking at face value. Remember, though, that *mezzo forte* is a dynamic range, so use this to colour the music, which shouldn't sound mechanical. The musical interest will be helped by clearly articulated phrasing as marked; short *staccato* notes and chords achieved by a vibrant finger/wrist *staccato* and clearly articulated couplets throughout are essential.

Crotchet = 152 is not as fast as you expect but don't go at 'counting speed'; this will result in a very lack-lustre performance. Instead, 'feel' the rhythm, particularly noting whether the five beats are subdivided two-and-three or three-and-two. Take note of the *vivo* marking, which gives the piece life and vitality.

There should be no *ritardando* at the end. Just stop.

GRADE 7

The majority of candidates at this level intend to get to Grade 8 and an accomplished performance of a Grade 7 programme will give real pleasure to the listener, including the examiner. The lists contain the various technical and musical challenges that might be expected but there are choices for those whose musical instincts outstrip their fingers, as well as ideal vehicles for budding virtuosi. As ever, it is the balance of strengths and weaknesses that goes to make the overall assessment, not the level of technical difficulty of the chosen piece. Teachers and candidates will know the wisdom and value of choosing a varied programme, as the all-round progress of the candidates preparing for an exam is arguably more important than the actual result on the day.

LIST A

The Handel is possibly the most approachable in the initial stages of preparation but needs an ear for line and good part-playing. The 'Allemande' by J. S. Bach also has demanding part-playing but is less of a high risk than the exciting movement from the sonata by C. P. E. Bach. This is certainly one for the technically confident, as is the finger-twisting allegro movement by Paradies. Most of the technical challenges lie in the rhythm of the Beethoven, with its two-against-three and three-against-four. The Scarlatti is inviting on the page but is physically less comfortable than it looks and needs expressive phrasing.

LIST B

The Chopin and Schumann will be familiar in style but both require largish hands for real ease in performance. The Moszkowski has a lovely melody but could lose its charm without careful balancing of the lines or *rubato*. The Granados would be a wise choice for those with a sense of colour and mood – the left-hand leaps are at a leisurely tempo. Born extroverts will go for 'Puck' but will need agility and stamina, as well as vitality and flair. The unusual Strauss 'Träumerei', once rhythmically understood, would be ideal for those with a gift for lyrical expressiveness.

LIST C

The 'Allegro Vivace' from Le Voleur d'Étincelles by Boutry and the Martinů piece are for the virtuosically inclined but are not beyond the more average player, given determination and persistent practice. Ravel's 'Prélude' needs an instinctive ear for pedal and sufficient patience to solve fingering difficulties and the right-hand octave passages. 'No. 2 from Hot Music' is ideal for those who like their jazz energetic and 'Sentimental Melody' is more suitable for those who enjoy the more reflective swung style. 'Memorial Blues' is fairly straightforward, providing that strong commitment to the mood is felt and conveyed.

A:1 Paradies *Allegro*

This is champagne music, a bubbling and fizzy *allegro* movement with a real sense of *joie de vivre* and, just like a good champagne, it needs good colour and vitality as well as plenty of character. It will suit those pupils who have shown an affinity with faster Scarlatti sonatas and are capable of sustaining clear, fast and light passage work.

Apart from a good excuse to do some important research into champagnes, use the opportunity of a page without dynamics to encourage pupils to decide their own. You will need to make decisions about the architecture of the piece but the broad rule of getting louder as the music ascends, softer as it descends, will be a good starting point.

This is unquestionably harpsichord music and, though it would be futile to expect the piano to sound like a harpsichord, do try to achieve a vibrant articulation in the semiquavers, without which the piece will sound rather lazy and heavy-footed. The quavers should be detached, with plenty of musical direction; imagine how a bassoonist might play them. Varying the degree of the *staccato* will help achieve some convincing shape and direction.

Technically the piece is something of a 'finger twister' and will suit the patient, conscientious student. There are lots of quick jumps and changes of clef so these will need careful attention and the fingering needs to be well-thought-out and consistent so that pupils don't find themselves stranded. Hesitations must be avoided at all cost, so the patterns and notes need thorough preparation and some passages memorized.

The suggested phrasing works extremely well, providing the pupil realizes that it is not to be taken too literally; a feeling of couplets and the slight extra emphasis this provides on the melodic note is all that is required. Do experiment with the phrasing though. The semiquaver figure on the second beat of bars 18–20 etc could well be phrased: three semiquavers slurred, final *staccato*; the descending arpeggio figures could be: two semiquavers slurred, two *staccato*. Hold the harmonic notes, as suggested in bars 2–5 in the right hand, to help the sense of line.

With confidence and security this is an unusual and exciting piece to perform and well worth the effort.

A:2 Beethoven *Vivace*

Many of us have the impression of Beethoven as a rather moody individual, falling out with his friends one day, showering them with love and praise the next. Beethoven's letters would make fascinating reading for an interested pupil. Most of us forget, however, that amidst his anger at his deafness and suffering due to constant ill-health there was a tremendous sense of humour. The more wicked side of Beethoven's humour certainly surfaces here, as not only is the movement full of smiles but I'm sure Beethoven would have looked on with some amusement as pupils and fellow musicians were caught out by the rhythmic games.

Don't be taken in. Each return of the rondo theme really will require some careful attention from even the most experienced of performers if the tempo is not to fluctuate. This said, the best overall approach to the piece is carefree and gay abandon, as only then does it have real fluency and conviction.

The opening is deceptively simple but returns in various guises and complexities. The more pompous and rather arrogant beginning to the second half of the rondo theme seems to laugh at us and challenge us to continue after every new difficulty that Beethoven throws in our way

Most of the technical problems consist of rhythmic and co-ordination difficulties, coupled with some fairly dramatic leaps towards the end. In the opening keep the left-hand chords as *legato* as possible, using pedal as appropriate (perhaps a dab on each beat in the first line but not at all in bars 9–12). The left-hand accompaniment in bars 18–20 needs quite a lot of rotation to provide sufficient tone and weight on the chords but, here and elsewhere, keep it light.

Don't be too afraid of bars 35 onwards. The best solution here is to let the hands get on with it but, as an orientation exercise, try playing only the first of each pair of semiquavers so that you end up with a simple quaver movement. Once used to this, see what happens. In the episode from bar 51 keep the chords light and give them musical direction. A gentle *crescendo* will work well. Notice the held notes in bars 67–71 which will provide more harmonic support.

Bars 80 onwards are easy, honest! As before, simply play the first and third semiquaver in the left hand and fit them two-against-three by duplicating the first right-hand note in the quaver rest. Finally, think of the first left-hand note as the first note in the right-hand triplet and away you go.

This is a joyful and fun-loving movement – enjoy it!

A:3 Handel *Allemande*

A wonderful allemande from the too-rarely played F minor suite. Allemandes are, by nature, serious dances and this one has some beautiful hidden melodies and delightful sequences. It might be interesting for a pupil to compare it with the allemande in the *C minor Partita* by Bach, or indeed any other Baroque allemande.

Avoid adopting too flippant a tempo or bouncy articulation. The crotchet = 76 is lively, although the piece will work as slow as crotchet = 60 without becoming too sentimental. Allow time to show the top line in the middle of bar 2 and throughout bar 3, where just a little more emphasis on the top notes will give a duet effect. Keep the semiquavers generally *legato* and barely detach the left-hand quavers, varying the degree to enhance the musical direction.

Give all the notes their full length; there is no need of pedal, so ensure that the fingering is thoroughly planned and rehearsed.

Bars 14–15 show how Handel wants us to listen to the semiquavers. Rather like the Bach cello suites, there are often two parts of importance in a single line. A listener should not be aware that the distribution of hands has changed here.

Explore the possible dynamic shape of the dance and use this to guide the listener through. Make a *decrescendo* perhaps in bars 3–4, then build up to the glorious heights of bar 7. Most importantly, don't accent the characteristic upbeat to the phrases; instead, make sure each melodic phrase has its own shape and colour.

The left-hand quavers work very well if you play all step-movement *legato* and separate all larger intervals, being careful to lighten the off-beat quavers in bars 5, 6 and similar bars. Show all the rests and allow just a little flexibility to the line.

Don't be afraid to lift the hands before the final chords of each section and then stylishly spread the chords, avoiding the common mistake of slowing at the end of the first section or taking too many beats before the second. A very small *rallentando* will enhance the final bar and provide a suitable ending to a charming and seductive movement.

A:4 C. P. E. Bach *Allegretto*

If your pupil can play the first eight bars at exactly the same tempo, there's a chance of success, and if this rhythmic security can be maintained at a reasonably brisk two-in-a-bar, then proceed with cautious optimism. Teachers will be well aware of the 'two tempo syndrome' – one for the easy bars and quite another for the demanding demisemiquavers, which in the wrong hands might be too heavy and laborious, losing tempo disastrously.

A certain amount of justifiable showing off is built into this little sonata movement. The deft execution of the scale passages is intended to give pleasure to the player and listeners, both by displaying musical grace but also as a means of relishing physical dexterity. Earlier background work on scales will prove its worth and the development of a key sense through scale practice will also pay dividends in providing a sense of direction to the dashing patterns.

Classical phrasing is at the heart of the style. Feminine endings at bars 4 and 8 establish the shapes and this form also gives structure to the demisemiquavers, which have just as much inherent expressiveness as the slower notes. Examiners often hear otherwise promising candidates go into machine-gun mode for florid passages, which may give startling articulation to each note but will not convey the musical content successfully.

A light finger touch helps these phrases to ripple along easily and they do actually lie comfortably under the hand, once mastered. An element of memory comes into play here, as the pace is too fast for individual notes to be read.

Structure should be presented with understanding by this stage and each section has an obvious start and end. Dynamic contrasts are marked and the natural rise and fall of the lines does the rest without too much extra attention. To really succeed, the piece must give an impression of being easily achieved, even though this is rarely the case in any performance.

There are some important passages where a certain amount of rotary freedom will come as a welcome relief and a chance to relax any tension (but not at the expense of the tempo). Bars 24–30, 44–46, 50–52 and 71–76 are all chances to let go of any forearm stress and prepare for the next bout of dexterity. The few ornaments are all at cadence points and could be simplified, if more adventurous flourishes upset the flow.

It's amusing to note that C. P. E. Bach put in only one fingering suggestion – a 1 at bar 81. Perhaps he thought the rest was obvious and to someone from his family it probably was! Most teachers will help their pupils by some additional 1s, around which so much of the fluency depends.

Once the piece is safely under the hands and in the system, it is well worth checking that the tempo at the end of the piece is still the same as the one set up in those vital first eight bars.

A:5 J. S. Bach *Allemande*

Despite its two pages of admirable visual clarity, this movement will take longer to learn than most pupils will expect. A last-minute rush will not give the chance for the intricacies to settle, so plan ahead with short, achievable targets. Four bars carefully assembled will be much more valuable for a week's work than a page sketchily practised.

Teachers will see the four-part writing and realize the challenges, where pupils will possibly only register two lines at a first glance. Try playing the top two parts, with the left hand taking the lower line. Then repeat the process with the lower two parts. This will immediately set up an awareness of holding the sustained parts, while keeping the clarity of the semiquavers. The next step is to work one hand at a time, aiming to produce the same effect as previously achieved with two. This detailed approach is likely to be accepted by pupils if only a short section is on the workbench at a time. It is also helpful for them to know what you expect to hear at the next lesson.

Ornaments, if included, need to be incorporated into the lines and learnt at the same time as the notes. The suggested decorations can usually be managed, as the tempo is fairly relaxed, but some of the left-hand mordents, especially on semiquavers, such as at bar 15, may be too demanding in an already complex corner. Ornaments giving emphasis to dotted quavers work well and should be started on the beat.

Phrasing could be rather elusive. The lines flow seamlessly forward and each of the two main sections is achieved by the gradual progress of shorter phrases, set up by the theme, which peaks at the first semiquaver of the second bar. This is then developed by different parts each having a similar balance. The editorial footnote suggests phrasing in short *legato* groups and some will choose this extra articulation. Many will play the whole theme *legato*, which is just as acceptable and possibly easier to achieve. Whatever you decide, the treatment of similar material later in the piece should be consistent.

Dynamics arise naturally from the harmonies and fluctuations of pitch. The pragmatic approach, which considers notes one week and dynamics the next, is not the ideal way forward; however, some planning will be needed for all but the most musically responsive.

The key structure is the foundation and the A minor start gives a gentle quality to the developing lines. Each four-bar phrase has its own shape, so it's a sensible plan to build gradually through each one – but not too strongly at this stage – then to drop down for the start of the next phrase. The first page reaches a more positive dynamic level with the arrival of the dominant E major key at bar 12. On the second page this is reversed, with a warm start then more subtle levels of tone, suggested by the flats and naturals around bar 14. The most assertive bars are at 22–23, where the distance between the hands is greatest (the third beat of bar 23). After this there is a rather sudden return to the tonic A minor, which relaxes the tension and brings the piece to a reflective conclusion.

The two essentials to have in mind when deciding on this allemande are reliable independence of part playing and the ability to give shape in a sensitive way to the four lines. Each part has a life of its own, which contributes its independent strength to the greater structure of the whole. Pupils who are familiar with teamwork will understand this concept quite readily.

A:6 D. Scarlatti *Sonata in F sharp*

'If only this were in F major!' Many pupils and perhaps teachers will have this thought, for the lack of semiquavers and the spare texture make this look quite simple – until you realize the physical impact of the key signature. This is not the time or place to muse about the possibility of playing it at Baroque pitch, a half-tone lower, tempting though this might be! We'll leave that for the purists and deal with the matter in hand: the key of F♯ major.

Putting aside any drawbacks for a moment, the beautiful, poised lines which express so much with such slim-line resources will appeal strongly to the ears, if not the fingers, and this is certainly a piece in which a teacher's demonstration can save many words in giving the right colour, tempo and style. For those short of time, the first 25 bars, then the middle section (bars 40–55) will be enough to give the right impression.

A strolling *andante* tempo works best but will only be graceful if the two-in-a-bar indication is felt. Four-in-a-bar would lose the elegance of the metre and limit the expressive possibilities. Starting as it does after a rest, the first main beat at bar 3 needs to be tactfully shown in the playing, but without a bump, as the piece really finds its rhythmic shape at the start of bar 4, then concludes the first phrase with a feminine ending at bar 7. This unusual phrasing, beginning halfway through the bar, is a feature of the entire piece and needs careful management of tone to avoid the impression of the bar lines being moved.

The middle section is a world away in key and colour. The suggested *forte* might be better translated as 'a warm sound', as this could easily be overdone and become harsh. The refinement of mood and style can be conveyed by the tone colour, rhythmic discipline and clean articulation of the lines. This is very civilized music and its essence may not be found by those in a hurry, or by good sight-readers (and there are some), who may skim through the notes without responding to what they are actually expressing.

To return to the practical front, the predominance of black keys makes the early learning stages a little precarious; slow, calm practice, relying on firm, clear fingerwork is therefore the first safe step. Ornaments are part of the style and, as the tempo is fairly leisurely, can be included without a scramble. The printed ones are stylish but feel free to adapt them or choose your own alternatives.

Terraced dynamics are very much a feature of this period and any repetitions make more of a point if they are played as 'echoes'. The edges between one dynamic level and a quieter one are sudden, like blocks of sound, but do this gently as the dynamics always need to be related to the atmosphere of the piece. The first obvious echo is from the third crotchet of bar 11 on to bar 14 and there are many similar possibilities for pupils to find for themselves. An idea for an aural test could be to spot these repetitions at a first hearing, when played by the teacher.

Some like their Scarlatti without any pedal; others like small touches to warm the sound and help the *legato*. Either approach will be equally acceptable but, if pedal is used, be careful not to extend this over any passages where there are semiquavers, as this would almost certainly blur the texture.

Examiners will notice with delight if the transition from the flats of the middle section melts sensitively into the returning sharps at bar 55, before setting off on the last part of the journey.

Rubato is not a word usually associated with Scarlatti and the basic beat is certainly constant. Musical players, however, will give tiny, affectionate touches to some corners, always within the beat, which will be unmistakable signs of stylistic and expressive awareness, rising far above the earlier hurdles presented by all those sharps.

B:1 Chopin *Mazurka in F minor*

Chopin wrote 31 mazurkas and this is one of his later ones. The dance is always in three-in-a-bar but look out for those characteristic accents on the second or third beats of a bar; this is where the male dancer is supposed to have tapped his heel or clapped his hands (bars 4, 9, 18 for example). Phrases also tend to end on the second beat of a bar and contain the characteristic dotted rhythm.

This mazurka contains many of the distinguishing features of the dance and will provide an excellent opportunity to explore the slightly elusive style. It is a serious dance, chromatic and slightly modal, but be careful the three beats don't seduce you into playing it like a waltz. It is in fact much more reflective and less light-hearted. The suggested tempo marking supports this and gives plenty of time to enjoy and shape all the wonderful melodic lines, many of which will need sensitively judged *rubato* and a true *legato*. The piece will suit a musical and assured pupil but will also need a fairly large hand for it to feel absolutely comfortable.

The piece falls neatly into three sections. The more cheery middle section yearns for just a little more movement and no examiner will object to this, unless overdone. Notice certain points of detail: firstly, the difference between the two dotted rhythms, those without rests in between (bar 4) and those with (bar 28). These need to be clearly contrasted, the quaver rest just allowing a little extra placing of the next main note. Secondly, show the accents but not too forcefully; keep them warm rather than percussive and place and hold them slightly as if going over a hump-backed bridge. Thirdly, keep all grace notes fairly much on the beat and, in bars 9, 41 etc, with the bass note.

The right-hand melody needs a singing *legato* touch but it is the left-hand accompaniment that will provide the greatest challenge. Light, *piano* chords, successively lighter as they go through the bar, need to be supported by a warm, rounded bass note which in turn will need to be held just a little longer to enable a gentle and effective change of the pedal. Listen carefully to the pedal changes and notice that there are some beats that would be far more effective without pedal. This applies in particular to the dotted rhythm with a rest and to the mordents.

The final 16 bars may seem at first sight to be a direct repeat of the first 16 but watch out for those typical and subtle Chopinesque changes to the harmony (E♮ in bar 41, an added C in bar 43 etc). Finish with a small *ritardando* and hold the final chord for its full two beats.

B:2 Schumann *Davidsbündlertanz*

Amongst Schumann's interests (apart from composing) were literature, champagne and girlfriends. He even wrote a whole set of variations based on one of his girlfriend's names. Just how much of each of his interests is reflected in this piece I shall leave for you to decide but Schumann's description *zart und singend* (tender and singing) points the way.

The date of the composition was also the year Schumann pledged himself to his beloved Clara Wieck but was refused permission to marry by her father, Schumann's former piano teacher. The piece seems to reflect a deep love and tenderness, so choose the tempo carefully. I'm more inclined to Clara's more pleading tempo but it must be a musical not a technical decision.

Think of the piece more as a song than a dance, allowing plenty of time for every imagined word and syllable to make its impact. To achieve the correct balance, imagine a song with cello and very light, flexible arpeggiated accompaniment. This will be fairly straightforward in the opening but will demand excellent listening and control later on, particularly when the melody is in the alto part. A lot of slow, listening practice is needed, getting used to an independence of tone not only between the two hands but also amongst the notes of one hand. Remember that the long, sustained melodic notes are decaying and the arpeggio figures will have to lighten and soften if they are not to become intrusive. All held and tied notes are significant and important in achieving the overall effect and in warming the harmonies. The tied grace notes in the melody in bars 2 and 4 come in just before the corresponding quaver.

As with much Schumann, smaller hands will have greater difficulty encompassing the many slightly awkward spans and stretches without a few bumps and blemishes. You can use plenty of pedal, changing each bar in the opening, but be a little more sparing in bars 21–24. Note the suggested distribution of the hands and don't be afraid to search for easier solutions.

Explore the most intimate and personal range of colour within each dynamic. Project the melody well, with plenty of tone, but draw the listener into the music with the most intense and beautiful shading of each phrase. The *piano* dynamic should not encourage a tentative approach. In the wrong hands this piece will sound metronomic and calculated but a musically inspired and tender performance will win the hearts and minds of even the most reluctant of audiences. If your pupil is unfamiliar with this style of music, ask them to listen to some recordings or, better still, take them to a concert.

B:3 Grieg *Puck*

Grieg was clearly well ahead of his time, establishing himself as one of the best fantasy writers, musically speaking, long before the current popular literature. This time it's that mischievous sprite Puck who gets the stage all to himself, causing mayhem amongst the human inhabitants of his territory before hiding back in his own underground world. Or so one possible story goes.

It's not just Puck who's being mischievous here though – it's Grieg as well. This piece needs the agility of an elf and the stamina of a goblin to play it, and if the key signature and accidentals haven't sent you into a spin and your pupil is a born extrovert then this is the piece to choose.

Actually the piece is not as hard as it sounds or looks; hands stay in the same relative position over the keys for bars at a time. Even in the middle section the right hand only jumps a few times and, otherwise, only the top note changes chromatically, making the reality far easier than the expectation.

The piece is going to rely on scintillating *staccato* chords (with the top notes brightened slightly with the finger), incisive accents, contrasting and exciting dynamics and a lot of energy and enthusiasm. Study and interpret the phrasing carefully and don't be scared to lift the hands off the keys at the ends of phrases, particularly in bars 11, 12, 13 etc.

Take the piece very slowly at first. Slow-motion performance practice is required – working at the sounds, colours and phrasing just as in the final performance, but slowly. Then speed it up bit by bit and just focus in on the one or two jumps and more awkward moments that let the performance down as you increase the tempo.

The opening *pianissimo staccato* in the left hand needs very active fingers from the surface of the keys. To get the right sound in the *staccato* chords 'grab' them from the surface of the key and use just a little arm weight and a relaxed wrist. The fingers will play an important role here, as any flabbiness or poorly judged balance (voicing) will result in a dull, casual sort of sound. Exaggerate all the dynamics in general and play with a smile. Barely any pedal is needed but use it where marked coming up cleanly with the hands at the end of a phrase.

Don't cheat on the four beats for the distant three o'clock bell (bars 49 onwards), which marks the moment for Puck to scamper back home, and 'rip' up the final right-hand quavers to the *sforzando* chord as the door swings shut.

B:4 Granados *Danza de la Rosa*

The pupil who will play this piece successfully will also be touched by the footnote. Granados' death at sea, whilst trying to save his wife after their ship had been torpedoed in 1916, will encourage respect and sympathy in sensitive pupils. This kind of information is far from irrelevant, as it not only engages the pupil's interest but also sets up an impression of the composer which will benefit the approach to his music, especially if it is a tender miniature like this little dance.

There is not much to add about this piece that has not already been indicated by Granados himself. The opening instructions 'Not lively and very simply, with rhythm', tell us quite a lot and the other musical details, dynamics, *rallentandi* and the last tempo change, are original, as is the pedalling.

Although the visual impression is straightforward, the tone quality is quite sonorous, especially on the second page with its low chords. Make sure these are caught securely with the pedal before moving the left hand quickly up to the ornamented second beat. A *cantabile* tone will sing the melody out clearly above the rich textures beneath. Most pupils find a *forte cantabile* the easiest to achieve but few manage the same quality at quieter dynamic levels.

Here a wide range of *cantabile* tone is needed; very gentle at the opening but still clearly defined, then much warmer at bars 17–26. The accented G at bar 27 is another request for an expressive singing sound, not a sudden punch, out of character with the rest of the piece. The gradual fading away from this *lento* bar to the end will only work if the start of the phrase is not too quiet. There must be somewhere left tonally to go. The final pedal holds the last three bars and, hopefully, can be released without an unplanned 'twang' as the dampers hit the strings.

Spanish music is usually quite strict in rhythmic shape and this, being a dance, has an almost hypnotic predictability to the left-hand chords. The decoration gives emphasis to certain beats, another characteristic Spanish flourish found also in their architecture and traditional clothing.

The left hand has quite large distances to cover, sometimes crossing over the right hand. The challenge here is to move faster than the actual tempo of the music, in order to ensure accuracy on arrival but not to appear rushed or awkward. Those with particularly short arms or, dare I say it, a rather bulky physique, may find this aspect enough to lead them to another choice. Most, however, will master the physical challenges with little trouble and will love the melody and mood. The sound management is an important consideration and the real fascination lies in finding the rich Mediterranean tone colours, while keeping the discipline of the dance.

B:5 Moszkowski *Calme du Soir*

Chords, whether calm or not, can often sound vertical and unconnected to a melodic line. It's not ideal to start with a negative thought when such a lovely piece is under scrutiny but going straight to the heart of the matter is always the fastest route towards real progress.

Playing the upper melodic line alone, then with the left-hand accompaniment, will quickly show what effect needs to be created when all the chords are in place. At least a week's practice doing just this will pay dividends and a demonstration of how awful this piece could sound when played thoughtlessly, without awareness of the *legato* melody, should halt even the most impatient pupils in their tracks and also inject some laughter into the lesson.

Although the inner harmonies are marked with dots, these are not *staccato* but are just gently detached. The upper line, where the melody lies, is always *legato* and needs lovely phrasing, regardless of what lies beneath.

The low bass notes at the starts of bars support the harmonies and it's important to catch these with the pedal, as marked. Teachers often ask at seminars if pedal can also be used where it's not marked and of course the answer is 'yes'. Lots of changes of pedal will be needed here and it would be well worth playing just the left hand plus pedal as a listening exercise. Once this is successfully managed, often with each quaver pedalled, the right hand can be safely added, knowing the foundation is in good order.

The obvious romanticism of the mood and period will find its way into the hearts of many pupils and this is also often the quickest route into the fingers. It's so much more rewarding to practise something you really enjoy.

The phrasing depends upon the ebb and flow. Plenty of flow towards the main points enables you to linger expressively without threatening the overall sense of direction. It is possible to pinpoint the peaks of phrases with great precision in earlier styles but in these salon pieces it is largely a matter of spontaneous response. With an exam on the horizon, such idealistic thoughts are not safe enough and most successful candidates will have been tactfully directed to the main points and so given clear destinations for their musical shaping.

The opening phrase could peak at the first quaver of bar 2, or could lean slightly on the F♯ at the end of the same bar. Once this shape is decided upon, there are similar patterns later in the piece.

On the second page, things become more dramatically charged and may well move on in tempo to the *agitato* of bars 17–18. This section contains the most taxing chords, which will need to be committed to memory for 100% safety in performance. This kind of writing is notoriously hard to pick up if the thread is lost and the physical memory, which is harder to establish with chords than with scale passages, needs to withstand the pressure of performance nerves.

From bar 19 to the end the music gradually relaxes into a mellow *legato* in all parts and the last few phrases sink gradually towards the home key of D major, all passion spent.

B:6 R. Strauss *Träumerei*

The ghost of Schumann seems to hover benevolently over this reverie. Both the title and the echoes of the *Prophet Bird* seem to imply connections with earlier pieces and it would be illuminating to play the Schumann items to your pupils before starting this untypical whim of Richard Strauss. He is so much more associated with vocal music, especially the opera *Der Rosenkavalier*, that it is a delightful surprise to find him almost improvising at the piano, with melodic lines at too high a pitch for even his favourite soprano.

Away from whimsy, although this does give the requisite colour and lightness of approach, the rhythm might be initially daunting. Pupils may need to hear a bar or so of the straight crotchets, feel the pulse, then relate this to the more complex sub-divisions with triplets and demi-semiquavers.

The *andantino* tempo indication is marvellous. Too fast and it becomes meaningless, too slow and the ideas will be earthbound. Successful freedom can only be found when there is a firm underlying rhythm; the various moments of flexibility, the commas, the improvisatory single melodic lines and the general pacing of the piece will not be overdone if the starting point is a clear sense of pulse and tempo.

The demisemiquavers need to be deft and light but beware of missing notes. Crisp fingerwork will ensure that each one speaks, however fleetingly. The upward arpeggio flourishes are played before the beat and sometimes split between the hands, with the left hand taking the top note. It's essential to look at the keys at these moments. Even professionals sometimes miss the mark in such exposed circumstances. There is an inevitable right moment to place these arpeggios, once the two crotchet chords of the previous bar have been played, also with their top notes forming the rhythm.

A very subtle range of tone colour needs to be created. The mood is all fantasy and the various instructions such as *zart*, meaning tender, give us the picture from the composer's own hand.

The technical demands of this piece are at least three-fold: the harp-like spread chords still need clarity, despite their gentleness; the solo melodic lines work best with *cantabile* tone in each hand and the right-hand groups of three demisemiquavers should keep their light definition.

A really communicative, atmospheric performance of this short piece will take us into another dimension for the minute or so that it takes to play. Let's hope we shall be able to travel far beyond the exam room.

C:1 Roger Boutry *Allegro Vivace*

This jewel thief is about to make his getaway, Keystone-Cops style. For those who are not familiar with the image then a trip to the video shop is in order.

Somewhat zany music, the piece conjures up the image of a police chase through crowded streets, horns hooting, bits falling off cars, impossible collisions and, of course, everyone all right in the end. The final 'phutt' from the robber's exhaust is in the last bar as the police cars close in.

Technically this piece will play itself once the notes are learnt. Notice that hands generally move in chords at the same time and simply need to know which notes to cover next. Practise, therefore, in chords and decide on your fingering. It is the stamina involved which will surprise and test a student. They really need to have tried a simple toccata or *mouvement perpétuel* to appreciate the physical and mental demands that will be all the easier if the piece is learnt from memory.

The first page will trundle away merrily but as hands get a little tired tension may begin to creep in, so a lot of slow, relaxed practice will be needed and, like a marathon runner, train over the distance occasionally but not necessarily at speed. Keep the arm light and balanced with just a little easy rotation of the hand in the opening and similar bars. From bar 26 onwards the hand needs to be much more still. The left hand needs a little more emphasis on the bottom notes and the chords kept light, but played with a comic bounce.

Treat the right hand in bar 17 as simple running semiquavers with little accents on the melodic notes (use the finger, not the arm). Then allow the pedal to hold the longer note. This will not work so well in bar 26 and onwards, where you will have to hold the dotted crotchet with the fingers in order to keep those wonderful left-hand chords *staccato*. In bar 25 jump quickly to the accented chord but then allow yourself just a little time to take a breath before resuming the chase.

The dynamics are very contrasted and will add a sense of drama to the performance. Don't include them as an afterthought; encourage them into the performance as you learn the notes. The sound you want will have a big influence on the technique and weight you use to play each passage.

Allow yourself plenty of time to coax the notes into the fingers and don't be in too much of a hurry to speed it up. It will soon begin to motor and be a real hit on the festival and concert circuit.

C:2 Copland *Sentimental Melody*

Brooklyn-born Aaron Copland was well acquainted with the jazz influences that were pervading all areas of music in the 1920s. He was also studying with one of Stravinsky's greatest admirers, Nadia Boulanger, and this strange mixing of styles is very apparent in this wonderful jazzy, yet contemporary-sounding, piece.

Copland is very particular about marking the triplets, which might imply that all other couplet quavers are straight. This will go against the grain with some more jazz-orientated pianists, who will instinctively want to swing all these rhythms. You will need to decide whether this is Classical music with jazz influence or the other way around.

The piece will suit a pupil who knows how to take time and enjoy harmonies and sentiment. A large stretch will help, as will a good ear for balance and line. Technically the left-hand part may inhibit a fluid performance if it is not well known and secure but notice that it is essentially bar 2 repeated a number of times with a few small variants. Once the left hand is familiar it will give plenty of time and space to explore the melodic interest of the right hand.

Don't be fooled by the lack of pedal markings. The pedal is definitely needed throughout. Show the left-hand rests in bars 8 and 9 but otherwise change each time the harmonies change.

The *sforzandi* should not be over-emphasized; it is merely Copland's way of indicating the convention of jazz musicians to slightly emphasize the final quaver of a swing rhythm. A few scales, three octaves in the following triplet rhythm: crotchet–quaver, crotchet–quaver, with accents on the quavers, or perhaps singing doo-*ba* doo-*ba*, will soon give the idea. Equally, don't squash the grace notes too severely or be too fussy over the numerous *tenuti* and accents; it is a slow, bluesy piece and all markings should be seen in this context, so go with the flow and interpret them as you instinctively feel is right.

Explore the full dynamic range within the piece and enjoy the music in a relaxed and slightly self-indulgent way: plenty of whispered asides and impassioned outbursts with lots of flexibility.

C:3 Ravel *Prélude*

This is a wonderfully reflective piece of music and should evoke the most tender and moving of emotions. Perhaps a landscape or a loved one comes to mind. There is plenty of warmth and sunshine tinged with just a hint of sadness but, like every special moment, it is to be savoured and enjoyed.

The first nine bars set the picturesque scene. A haunting pentatonic tune then enters – perhaps a distant shepherd's flute heard drifting across the hills and coloured by the misty chromaticism in the left hand. A sunshine warmth begins to brighten the prelude from bar 16 and the piece ends slightly questioning and uncertain.

The image is a fleeting one. The piece is one of the shortest from list C but if it sounds like a waltz then it is decidedly too short and too fast. Take the *Assez lent* quite seriously and note all the other tempo markings throughout the piece.

The first two phrases work well if thought of in one long breath, the third phrase reinforcing the idea. In the middle section balance the octaves sensitively and follow Ravel's dynamic indications to shape the line. Notice that the loudest dynamic in the piece is *piano*, so don't choose too tentative a tone; there is *pianissimo* to follow and you may even wish for more flexibility in the pianistic colours you choose.

Technically the piece is fairly self-explanatory. Project the top notes of the chords and keep the line *legato* to permit judicious and subtle changing of the pedal where required. The accompanying left-hand figures will require a little more weight at the bottom and to be shaped physically and musically almost as a gesture.

The middle section is probably the most awkward as the hands are inclined to get into something of a tangle. Bring the left hand over the right and keep the thirds light and very *legato*, allowing the melody through. The suggested fingering is appropriate and effective here but will need some gentle persuading before it will feel familiar. Larger hands will find the octaves slightly easier and will be able to finger the top notes to achieve a good *legato*.

Put the pedal down with the bottom note of each arpeggio figure but thereafter use your ears to judge whether to change a little more frequently to avoid too much confusion in the sound and harmonies. Consider whether to hold the pedal down for the whole of the final four bars or perhaps to half-pedal. Do try some *una corda* in the middle section.

The ending is very beautiful yet unresolved. Hold the pause for a good length and then notice the rests. Ravel doesn't want you to move a muscle well beyond the final note as the image becomes less focused and finally fades away.

C:4 Gabriel Jackson *Memorial Blues*

Phyllis Hyman, who died in 1995, was a Rhythm and Blues singer of 'haughty sensuality' – an interesting combination of qualities which, not surprisingly, also applies to this sophisticated blues.

Although the bar lengths are unequal, the few funereal crotchets have dignity and regularity. The single notes of the right-hand melodic lines have been grouped to imply an improvised style and, rhythmically precise though these appear, they can convey a female singer's mournful wail if given the right feel and *cantabile* sound.

The different sections are punctuated by commas and the timing of these corners can add considerable poise and impact to the performance. They also give a valuable moment in which to prepare for the next tone colour. Sound has to be imagined – heard with the inner ear – before the physical approach can follow and, at this stage, pupils will probably be reasonably familiar with the idea of drawing different sounds from the piano, not just 'doing the dynamics'.

The chordal passages, especially those lower on the keyboard, need a rich sonority with no hard edges. Relaxed shoulders and arms will help to get this 'nightclub' colour. It is still possible to keep the hands exactly together and make a *legato* line of the procession.

At the bottom of the first page, several interesting new ideas emerge. First there is a 3/8 bar in which a low 'pedal point' chord is put down with both hands, caught with the pedal, then sustained for six bars. The semi-quavers, also split between the hands, add an almost bell-like element, with their rhythmically crisp and bright patterns. Bar 39, with its five quavers, will need careful counting as the low chord is repeated at this point. Covering the distance from bass to treble must be done swiftly here, or the 5/8 bar could well gain an extra quaver.

Combined ideas at bar 54 create an atmospheric coda. It's wise to keep the rhythm taut, as instructed by the composer, right up to the last chords, where there is a written-out *rallentando*, made by the increasing time values. The last chord, with hands very wide apart, should sound dignified, poised and extremely final.

C:5 Martinů *What shall we play now? Tag?*

Question marks, two of them in this title, can alter the entire tone of the words they follow. So it is here, and awareness of the lightness implied by the title can not only set the right atmosphere but also directly affect the playing technique.

At first glance, the almost military precision and relentless flow of the quavers, plus the *sempre staccato* indication, seem to require exuberant energy and finger attack akin to machine-gun fire. The first quality is essential – the infectious vitality of children, almost out of control in the *accelerando* phrases, must be part of the performance. The finger articulation, however, is not at all aggressive and needs a crisp lightness, even at the louder dynamic levels.

Most pupils will prefer to have the right hand over the top of the left and it's worth noticing that the right hand leads the beat almost throughout, except at bars 41–46 and the final passage. The lower part is *sotto voce* at the start and is nearly always the subservient partner.

The obvious trap lies in inadvertently changing the rhythm in the effort to achieve a reasonable tempo. There should be four equal quavers per bar. The first is the strongest, then beats two and four follow more lightly. All too easily, this could sound more like a crotchet–quaver pattern, if the hands are not co-ordinated exactly. Once the even patter of quavers is established, the next step is to practise them at all the different dynamics marked, while still keeping the tempo and evenness. At this grade there may still be a tendency to lose tempo when playing at the quieter levels. Keeping physically close to the keys gives a much greater control and feeling of safety.

The *poco allegro* at the start warns us to keep an eye on the speedometer, as there is a faster tempo to come at the *allegro vivo* on the second page. Just how fast this goes is a matter for the individual player but it should be noticeably more exciting than the tempo at the start.

The two minim chords at bars 48–49 give a chance to catch our breath before a completely different tempo and mood arrive with the *moderato* section. Pedal will probably be used by most players here and the upper chords need finger connection and an extra squeeze on the outside line to give melodic definition. The suggested finger changing on the repeated left-hand B♭ is a textbook idea but seems perverse and likely to draw too much attention to this line. Do whatever comes naturally here, as there are more important considerations than this detail.

The four-bar phrases are given plenty of clear instructions from the composer. We know what he wants but must convey this while keeping the mood happy, naïve and yet excited. It would be a shame to play this delightful party piece with a fierce frown and gritted teeth. Looking relaxed while doing something challenging is also worth practising.

C:6 Erwin Schulhoff *No. 2 from Hot Music*

Almost from Grades 1 and 2, it's now possible to swing along with the Board these days. Many pupils love the relaxed, jazzy styles, which are often more rhythmically demanding than the straight classical choices. The sugar sweetens the pill. It's your choice whether or not to swing this particular piece or play the dotted quaver–semiquaver patterns as written.

There is no advantage either way in an exam but each will need rock-like rhythmic accuracy in the fundamental beat. Bars that start with rests need extra care; watch bars 9–10, a trap for the unwary that may need initial counting in quavers to find exactly which chord goes on which beat. Once this is intellectually understood and absorbed, the brain needs to be put aside in favour of instinct and a feel for the idiom.

The right physical approach always helps the sound and, although some jazz players take their 'groovy' posture to extremes, a certain relaxation will be necessary both for the right tone colour – punchy at the *forte* chords but not harsh – and also to avoid the 'serious pianist attempting jazz' look of the performance.

Of course, examiners will not comment on the way a candidate looks at the piano but this will have an impact on the performance itself in various subtle ways. Sitting too close to the keyboard or having a rigidly straight back will seriously inhibit this kind of piece.

The accents are all there for a reason and feeling why they work is at least as important as dutifully observing them and bringing them out at the right moments. Pedal should be extremely economical; a kind of relaxed clarity is very much a part of this style, not to be sacrificed by a false feeling of safety when the right foot goes down in moments of stress.

This piece should be played up to speed throughout; the suggested indication of minim = 100 is ideal. Please don't misread the minim beat for a crotchet – it's surprising the number of pupils who do. The right hand holds the final D atmospherically, long after the last left-hand C has dropped onto the night-club floor.